Start a Business in 10 Minutes a Day

A Guide for Busy People: Launch a Startup in Minutes a Day with Minimal Stress (with daily 100-point step by step checklist)

Andre St Pierre

Publisher: Urban Cabin Collection

ISBN (Paperback): 978-1-0692940-3-6

ISBN (Hardcover): 978-1-0692940-0-5

ISBN (eBook): 978-1-0692940-5-0

Contents

Start Small, Dream Big

Starting a business might seem like a daunting mountain to climb, especially if your schedule is already packed to the brim. Between work obligations, family commitments, and the relentless demands of daily life, the thought of launching your own startup can feel like a far-off dream—one reserved for people with more time, money, or experience. But what if I told you that you don't need to overhaul your life or wait for the "perfect moment" to start a business?

What if you could do it in just 10 minutes a day?

This book is your guide to turning that dream into reality. It's not about working harder or sacrificing more; it's about working smarter and breaking the journey into manageable, bite-sized steps. Over the next 20 days, we'll work together to transform your idea into a real, tangible business—one 10-minute session at a time.

Setting Expectations

Let's start by setting some clear expectations. First, understand that this process is designed to fit into your busy life, not disrupt it. Each step is crafted to be achievable within 10 minutes, making progress steady and sustainable. Some days, you'll make big leaps, and other days, it will be about refining small but crucial details. Either way, every step forward matters.

Second, recognize that perfection isn't the goal here. Progress is. You're not expected to have all the answers right away or to create a flawless business on day one. This is a learning journey, and it's okay to make mistakes along the way. In fact, mistakes are valuable; they teach you what works, what doesn't, and how to improve. Embrace them as part of the process.

Finally, remember that success doesn't look the same for everyone. For some, it might mean creating a side hustle that generates extra income. For others, it could be the first step toward financial freedom. Define what success means to you, and let that vision guide your efforts.

Be Open to Learn and Grow

Starting a business is as much about personal growth as it is about professional success. Each step in this book will challenge you to think creatively, step outside your comfort zone, and develop new skills. Along the way, you'll learn about marketing, sales, branding, and more. But perhaps the most important lesson is this: every entrepreneur starts as a beginner. The key is to stay curious, be adaptable, and commit to continuous learning.

Mistakes are inevitable, but they're also opportunities in disguise. Didn't get the response you wanted from a potential customer? That's valuable feedback to refine your pitch. Chose a logo design that didn't resonate? Now you know what doesn't work. The goal is not to avoid mistakes but to learn from them and keep moving forward.

Celebrate the Journey

Launching a business is an incredible accomplishment, no matter how big or small it might seem. Every time you complete a step, no matter how small, take a moment to acknowledge your progress. Share your wins with family and friends; their support and encouragement can be a powerful motivator. Whether it's choosing a business name, designing your first logo, or making your first sale, each milestone is a reason to celebrate.

Remember, the journey is just as important as the destination. Entrepreneurship isn't just about building a business; it's about building yourself—your confidence, your skills, and your ability to create something meaningful. So enjoy the process, savor the victories, and don't forget to look back and appreciate how far you've come.

Let's Get Started

By the time you finish this book, you'll have taken your idea and transformed it into a fully launched business.

The best part?

You'll have done it without feeling overwhelmed, sacrificing your personal life, or burning out. All it takes is 10 minutes a day, a willingness to learn, and the courage to take that first step.

I am excited to be on this journey with you as your guide. Starting with just 10 minutes a day you can build a highly successful business and start to work toward financial freedom. So grab your notebook, set a timer for 10 minutes, and let's get to work.

Your business—and your future—awaits!

CHAPTER 1

Preparing for Your
Business Journey

Understanding Your Why

This first chapter will include some self-reflection, goal setting and the start of a wonderful, exciting and thrilling journey toward your new business. We can probably agree that we would like to make a healthy living and earn money to provide for ourselves, our families and ensure a high quality of life.

Those are admirable goals but what else is driving you?

This is an important aspect to understand as we begin this epic adventure!

Define Your Motivation for Starting a Business

Starting a business isn't just about creating a product or offering a service—it's about pursuing a vision that aligns with your values, passions, and goals. Whether you're looking for financial independence, creative freedom, or the opportunity to make an impact, understanding *why* you're starting a business is crucial for staying motivated and navigating the inevitable challenges ahead. By defining your motivation, you create a deeper connection to your business, which will keep you driven and focused on your long-term success.

1. Identify Personal and Professional Goals

One of the first steps in defining your motivation is understanding the **personal and professional goals** that are driving you. Why are you venturing into entrepreneurship in the first place? Is it a desire to break free from the traditional 9-to-5 grind? Or is it the opportunity to create something meaningful and scale it into a successful venture?

Here are some personal and professional goal categories to consider:

- **Financial Independence:** For some, the motivation to start a business is rooted in the desire to achieve financial freedom. You may want to generate income that isn't tied to a salary or develop a business that allows you to build wealth over time.

- **Work-Life Balance:** Many entrepreneurs are motivated by the flexibility and control that comes with owning a business. You might be seeking a lifestyle where you can work on your own terms, prioritize your family, or travel without being tied to a traditional office schedule.

- **Creative Expression:** If you're passionate about a specific field, starting a business can be a way to express your creativity and share your unique vision with the world. Whether it's writing, art, design, or another area of passion, a business gives

8

you the opportunity to turn that passion into a profession.

- **Impact and Legacy:** Some entrepreneurs are motivated by the desire to make a difference. Your goal may be to create a business that solves a problem or addresses a social issue. Building something that leaves a positive legacy can be a powerful motivator for long-term success.

Consider both your **personal** and **professional** motivations to get a full picture of what you're hoping to achieve. Knowing what you want from both aspects of your life will help you set clear goals and create a roadmap for achieving them.

2. Connect Your Business Idea to Your Passions

When you align your business with your passions, you set yourself up for success—not just financially, but personally. Passion fuels persistence, and the deeper the connection you feel to your business, the more likely you are to stay committed through tough times.

Ask yourself:

- **What excites you?** What aspects of your business idea light a fire within you? It could be the product itself, the industry, or the opportunity to solve a problem for others.

- **What skills or knowledge do you already have?** Often, your business idea will stem from your expertise, experience, or personal interests. If you have a passion for fitness, starting a health coaching business might feel natural. If you love technology, developing an app or offering digital services could be a perfect fit.

By connecting your business to your passions, you're more likely to stay engaged and energized. This connection will also resonate with your customers, as your enthusiasm and commitment will shine through in your marketing and interactions. Passion is contagious, and when you believe in what you do, others are more likely to believe in it too.

3. Clarify Your Long-Term Vision

Having a **long-term vision** is crucial when starting a business, especially when the initial stages can be overwhelming. Your vision provides a sense of purpose and direction, helping you make decisions that align with your overarching goals.

Here are some questions to help you clarify your vision:

- **Where do you see your business in 5 or 10 years?** Do you envision growing a multi-location enterprise, running an online business that reaches global audiences, or building a personal brand that is recognized in your field?

- **What kind of impact do you want to have?** What do you want your business to represent? This could be the quality of the products or services you offer, the culture you create within your company, or the broader societal or environmental impact you hope to make.

- **What lifestyle do you want to create?** Consider how your business will integrate with your personal life. Do you want to scale quickly and hire a team, or are you aiming for a small, manageable business that provides flexibility and freedom?

Clarifying your long-term vision helps you stay focused on the bigger picture. It provides a guiding star to return to when things get tough, keeping you grounded in the purpose behind your business. Your vision is what makes the everyday hustle worthwhile—it's the "why" that fuels your "how."

By defining your motivation early on—both personal and professional—connecting your business to your passions, and establishing a long-term vision, you're laying the foundation for sustainable success. Having a clear sense of motivation will help you stay on track, even when the journey gets challenging. When you align your business with your values and aspirations, you're more likely to push through obstacles and stay committed to achieving your goals.

"Every step forward is a victory."

Assess Your Current Lifestyle and Time Availability

Starting a business can feel like a daunting task, especially when you're already juggling other responsibilities. However, it's possible to make steady progress by aligning your business efforts with your current lifestyle and time availability. The key is to **break things down into manageable chunks** and **work consistently**, even if it's just for 10 minutes a day. Here's how to assess your current situation and plan your time effectively.

1. Identify Your Busiest Periods

To make room for building your business, it's important to understand when you are the busiest. This will help you plan around your other commitments and avoid feeling overwhelmed.

Ask yourself:

- **When do I have the least amount of time?** Are there certain times of the day or specific days of the week when your schedule is packed, like mornings before work, evenings after family commitments, or weekends with errands? Knowing when you're least available will help you avoid unrealistic expectations.

- **What periods can I dedicate to focused work?** Similarly, consider when you have pockets of time that can be devoted to your business. Perhaps you have a few quiet moments during your lunch break, some time after the kids are asleep, or a calm weekend morning. Identifying these "golden hours" will allow you to take advantage of even the smallest windows of opportunity.

- **Factor in your energy levels:** Your time availability is important, but so is your **energy**. Think about when you're at your best: Are you a morning person who feels most energized at the start of the day? Or do you thrive at night, when the world is quieter? Schedule your 10-minute sessions during your peak energy periods to maximize focus and productivity.

By identifying your busiest times and the best moments for focused work, you can plan ahead to ensure you're using your available time as efficiently as possible.

2. Plan for Dedicated 10-Minute Sessions Daily

The beauty of starting a business in 10-minute sessions is that **small, consistent actions** add up over time. Even if you feel like you don't have hours each day, committing to just 10 minutes of focused work every day can lead to significant progress.

To make this work for you:

- **Set clear goals for each session:** With only 10 minutes, it's important to be focused. Break down your to-do list into manageable chunks, and commit to completing one task during each session. For example, one day you might focus on brainstorming your business name, while another day you could work on your elevator pitch.

- **Create a daily routine:** Incorporate your 10-minute sessions into your existing routine, so it doesn't feel like an added burden. For example, set aside 10 minutes in the morning before you start your day, during your lunch break, or right before you go to bed. Making it a habit ensures you stay consistent.

- **Track your progress:** Keep a simple checklist or journal to track your daily 10-minute sessions. This will not only give you a sense of accomplishment but also help you stay motivated as you watch your business take shape day by day.

Remember, the goal is consistency, not perfection. Every little action adds up, and over time, these 10-minute sessions will accumulate into real, measurable progress.

3. Recognize Potential Challenges

While the 10-minute approach is designed to minimize overwhelm, it's important to acknowledge potential challenges that could interfere with your ability to make time for your business. By recognizing these challenges upfront, you can plan for them and take steps to overcome them.

Some potential challenges include:

- **Distractions or interruptions:** Life is busy, and interruptions can happen. If you're working from home or juggling multiple responsibilities, distractions are inevitable. To combat this, create a designated time and space for your business work where you can minimize distractions. Consider setting up a quiet workspace and using tools like noise-canceling headphones or a "Do Not Disturb" signal to stay focused.

- **Feeling overwhelmed by other commitments:** When juggling family, a job, or other personal responsibilities, it's easy to feel like there's not enough time for everything. Be kind to yourself, and recognize that some days you may need to adjust or even skip your 10-minute session. Don't let one missed session derail your progress.

- **Staying motivated over time:** In the beginning, it's easy to stay excited, but as you move forward, motivation can fluctuate. One way to keep your momentum going is to revisit your initial **motivation** for starting your business— remind yourself of your personal and professional goals, and the reason you're building this business in the first place. If you feel stuck, try changing up your routine or working on a different aspect of your business to keep things fresh.

By anticipating these challenges, you'll be better prepared to handle setbacks and stay on track.

Set Realistic Expectations for Success

Starting a business is an exciting journey, but it's important to set **realistic expectations** from the get-go. While you might dream of rapid success, the path to building a thriving business is often filled with small steps, adjustments, and learning experiences. By embracing the process and celebrating your progress, you'll stay motivated and build momentum over time. Here's how to set the right expectations and keep moving forward with confidence.

1. Acknowledge Small Wins Along the Way

In the early stages of your business, progress can feel slow. You might not see immediate financial returns, or your marketing campaigns might not take off as quickly as you hoped. But remember, **every step forward is a victory**, no matter how small. Acknowledging these wins helps you stay positive and focused on the journey rather than just the destination.

Small wins could include:

- Successfully registering your business name.
- Completing your first product prototype.

- Getting positive feedback from a potential customer or client.

- Finishing a major milestone, like setting up your website or opening a business bank account.

- Reaching a small sales target or launching your first ad campaign.

Celebrating these milestones boosts your confidence and reminds you that **progress is progress,** no matter the pace. It also helps you stay energized when challenges arise, as you can look back and see all that you've accomplished.

2. Understand the Iterative Nature of Startups

One of the key lessons to embrace when starting a business is that success rarely happens in a straight line. Building a startup is an **iterative process,** meaning it involves repeated cycles of trial and error, testing, and refining. You'll continuously tweak and improve your ideas, products, and strategies until you find what works best for your audience.

Here's why this iterative nature is important:

- **Feedback is invaluable:** Every time you test an idea or launch something new, you gather valuable insights. If something doesn't go as planned, it's an opportunity to learn and adjust your approach. Don't view mistakes or failures as setbacks; they're stepping stones that bring you closer to your goal.

- **Pivoting is part of the process:** You might find that the original idea you had needs to be adjusted based on market feedback, personal experience, or new trends. This is perfectly normal. Successful startups often pivot—change direction, tweak their products, or alter their business model as they learn more about what their audience truly needs.

- **Growth takes time:** Even if your product or service is solid, building a customer base, increasing brand awareness, and generating steady revenue can take time. Be patient and remember that **the most successful businesses were not built overnight**—they were built over years of iterative work, with consistent improvements and adaptations.

Accepting the reality of an iterative process allows you to move forward with confidence. You won't get discouraged when things don't go perfectly the first time; instead, you'll see them as opportunities to fine-tune your approach and get closer to success.

3. Embrace a Mindset of Progress Over Perfection

One of the biggest traps aspiring entrepreneurs fall into is the desire for **perfection**. It's tempting to think that your business must be flawless before you can launch it or market it to the world. But the truth is, **progress always trumps perfection**.

Here's why embracing progress is so important:

- **Done is better than perfect:** Launching your business with something that's "good enough" is far better than waiting for everything to be perfect. Your business will evolve over time, and the sooner you start, the sooner you can learn what works—and what doesn't. Perfectionism often leads to paralysis by analysis, where you get stuck trying to make everything perfect and never move forward.

- **Speed and action breed results:** By focusing on making progress—however small—you can move through the startup process quickly. Whether it's launching a website, offering your first service, or getting customer feedback, the sooner you act, the more information you gather. This feedback is what drives growth and helps you improve your product or service.

- **Imperfections make you human:** When you embrace imperfection, it can actually work in your favor. Customers are often drawn to authenticity, and showing that you're evolving as a business adds a human touch. No one expects a new business to be perfect—what they expect is real value, transparency, and a willingness to improve.

Focusing on **progress over perfection** helps you avoid the trap of procrastination and gives you the confidence to move forward, even if things aren't perfect yet. Every step you take is a building block for the future success of your business.

Choosing the Right Business Idea

Things will really start to get exciting for us now! This is a critical part in your journey and don't forget, one of the strengths of a business owner is the ability to pivot and adjust on the fly. If you are concerned you may not have that skill just yet, that's ok - you will learn!

Brainstorm Ideas Aligned with Your Interests and Skills

The foundation of a successful business often lies in **pursuing something you're passionate about** and **leveraging your existing expertise**. When your business idea aligns with your personal interests and skills, you'll not only find it easier to stay motivated but also more enjoyable to build and scale. This section will help you brainstorm business ideas that fit with what you love to do and are rooted in areas where you already have expertise.

1. Reflect on Your Hobbies and Expertise

The first step in brainstorming business ideas is to take a deep dive into your **hobbies, skills, and**

passions. Think about what you enjoy doing in your free time, the activities that energize you, and the areas where you excel. Often, the best business ideas emerge from the things you're naturally drawn to.

Here's how to reflect on your personal interests and expertise:

- **What do you love doing?** Start by listing your hobbies and activities that bring you joy. Whether it's cooking, fitness, writing, painting, or organizing, these personal interests can spark ideas for a business that you'll love running every day.

- **What are you good at?** Consider your professional background, education, and any specific skills you've developed over the years. Do you have a knack for graphic design? Are you an excellent communicator? Do you have expertise in a specific industry? Leveraging these skills can help you build a business where you can hit the ground running.

- **What do others come to you for help with?** Another way to uncover your expertise is to think about the advice or services people often ask you for. If your friends frequently ask for career advice, maybe consulting or coaching is the right path. If people turn to you for recipe ideas or gardening tips, perhaps there's a business opportunity in the food or home and garden industry.

By tapping into your own passions and expertise, you create a business foundation that feels authentic and sustainable. When you're passionate about what you do, the work becomes enjoyable, and you're more likely to stick with it during the tough times.

2. Research Trending Markets and Opportunities

While your personal interests and expertise are vital, it's equally important to ensure that there's a **market demand** for your business idea. Researching trends and emerging markets will give you insight into where there is potential for growth and what consumers are looking for.

Here's how to research trending markets and opportunities:

- **Check out industry reports and forecasts:** Many industry publications, such as those from Nielsen, Statista, and IBISWorld, offer in-depth insights into emerging trends across various sectors. These reports can help you spot growing industries, rising consumer behaviors, and lucrative opportunities.

- **Follow blogs, podcasts, and social media:** Stay up-to-date on the latest trends by following relevant blogs, podcasts, YouTube channels, and social media influencers in your area of interest. Websites like Medium, Reddit, and LinkedIn often feature the latest insights from industry experts and thought leaders, giving you a sense of what's gaining traction in the market.

- **Look for gaps in existing products/services:** One of the best ways to identify a trend is by observing **what's missing** or under-served in the current market. Are there pain points in a popular industry that aren't being addressed? Are customers looking for a better solution to a problem? These gaps could reveal an opportunity for your business.

- **Analyze competitors:** Study businesses in your target market to understand what they're doing well and where they might be falling short. Read customer reviews, see what people like and dislike about existing offerings, and look for areas of improvement. This will not only help you spot opportunities but also allow you to refine your business concept to offer something new or better.

By researching current market trends, you ensure that your business idea isn't just based on personal passion but also has the potential for demand and growth in the real world.

3. Identify Gaps You Can Fill

A critical step in brainstorming business ideas is identifying the **gaps in the market** that your business can fill. This is where your creativity, research, and expertise will come together. Start by identifying problems that your target audience is facing and think about how you can solve them in a unique and valuable way.

Here's how to spot market gaps:

- **Focus on customer complaints:** Look for products or services that people complain about. Whether it's a product with poor quality, a service that lacks customer support, or a pain point that isn't addressed by current solutions, these are opportunities for you to innovate and offer something better.

- **Think about your own frustrations:** Reflect on your own experiences as a consumer. Is there a product or service you've used that you wish worked differently? Can you design a better version or offer a solution that addresses these issues? Many successful businesses were born from the frustration of their founders with existing offerings.

- **Examine underserved niches:** Explore underserved niches or customer segments that are overlooked by larger businesses. This could be a specific demographic (like seniors, remote workers, or busy parents), a geographic area, or a subcategory within an industry. Serving a niche market can help you stand out and create a loyal customer base.

- **Survey your target audience:** If you're unsure about the gaps in the market, consider surveying potential customers to get their feedback. Ask questions about their needs, challenges, and desires. This will provide valuable insights that you can use to shape your business offering.

By identifying a market gap and crafting a solution, you position your business as a provider of value, and this can give you a competitive edge as you move forward.

"Progress always trumps perfection."

Validate Your Business Idea

Before investing time and money into your business, it's crucial to **validate your idea** to ensure there's a real demand for what you plan to offer. This step helps you minimize risk, refine your concept, and ensure that you're building something your audience actually wants. Fortunately, validating a business idea doesn't require a large investment or months of work—you can start the process in **just a few minutes a day**. Here's how to quickly validate your idea.

1. Conduct Quick Online Research

The first step in validating your business idea is to do some **basic online research**. The internet is a goldmine of information, and a few hours of digging can give you valuable insights into whether your idea has potential.

Here's how to conduct your research:

- **Search for existing solutions:** Begin by searching for similar businesses or products. See if others are already offering something like your idea and how successful they seem to be. Check reviews, ratings, and comments to learn what customers like and dislike. A saturated market doesn't necessarily mean your idea is bad—it could simply indicate that there's demand, and you might need to differentiate yourself.

- **Analyze industry reports:** Look for reports, articles, or case studies about the market or industry your business falls into. Websites like Statista, Google Trends, and industry-specific publications can provide insights into current market conditions, growth projections, and emerging trends. This will help you understand whether the market is expanding or stagnating and how much competition you're up against.

- **Explore online forums and social media:** Platforms like Reddit, Quora, or Facebook Groups are valuable for understanding what people are saying about products and services in your niche. Join relevant groups or search keywords related to your business idea to see what questions or problems people are discussing. If your idea aligns with these discussions, it could be a sign of demand.

Quick online research gives you a clear understanding of the market landscape and helps you fine-tune your business concept before moving forward.

2. Use Surveys or Polls to Gather Feedback

One of the best ways to validate your business idea is by getting direct **feedback from potential customers.** Surveys and polls are simple and quick ways to gauge interest and identify pain points. With tools like Google Forms, SurveyMonkey, or even Instagram polls, you can gather useful data to validate your idea.

Here's how to use surveys and polls effectively:

- **Create a simple questionnaire:** Design a short survey that focuses on key aspects of your business idea. Ask questions that will give you insights into customer needs, preferences, and pain points. Some example questions might include:

  - "Would you be interested in a product that solves [specific problem]?"

  - "How much would you be willing to pay for a service that does [feature]?"

  - "What are the biggest challenges you face with [problem your business solves]?"

- **Distribute your survey:** Share your survey with your target audience. If you have an email list, social media following, or access to relevant groups, start by sending it there. You can also use paid ads on platforms like Facebook or Instagram to target specific demographics and get more responses. The more feedback you gather, the better.

- **Analyze the results:** After collecting responses, look for patterns in the data. Do people seem interested in your idea? Are there specific features or offerings that are particularly appealing? If you receive a lot of positive feedback, you're on the right track. If responses are lukewarm or negative, use this information to refine or pivot your idea.

Surveys and polls are a great way to get **direct, actionable feedback** from your target audience, allowing you to validate your business idea with real data.

3. Test Demand with a Simple Experiment

Once you've done your research and gathered feedback, the next step is to test the **demand for your business** with a **low-cost, low-risk experiment.** This is where you can really see if people are willing to pay for your product or service.

Here are a few simple experiments you can try:

- **Pre-sell your product or service:** Create a landing page or simple website that explains your product or service and offers people the chance to buy or sign up for updates. Even if your product isn't fully developed, offering a "pre-order" option can test if customers are willing to pay for it in advance. This gives you concrete evidence of demand before you invest time in production.

- **Create a minimum viable product (MVP):** If you have a product idea, create a **minimal version** of it that you can sell or show to customers. This could be a prototype, a sample, or a simple version of the service. For example, if you're launching an app, create a basic version with just a few features and see if users are interested. If they are, you can expand it based on their feedback.

- **Run a small ad campaign:** If you're offering a product or service online, consider running a small Facebook or Google ad campaign to see if people click and convert. Create a simple ad and direct people to a landing page where they can learn more or sign up. Even a small budget can give you a good indication of whether there's enough interest.

These **real-world tests** give you real-time data and show you if your idea has the potential to succeed. Testing demand early in the process allows you to make informed decisions and avoid wasting resources on an idea that may not resonate with your audience.

Validating your business idea is a crucial step in ensuring that your time and resources are spent wisely. With quick online research, feedback from your target audience, and simple demand tests, you can determine whether your idea has potential and make any necessary adjustments before diving in fully. By validating your idea early, you reduce the risk of failure and increase the likelihood of building a successful business.

Ensure Your Idea Aligns with Your Available Resources

Before diving headfirst into your business idea, it's essential to **assess whether you have the**

resources—financial, skill-based, and time-related—to bring it to life. Aligning your idea with your available resources will not only help you avoid overwhelm but also set you up for success from the beginning. This section will guide you through evaluating your startup costs, leveraging your skills, and focusing on a **minimum viable product (MVP)** to get started efficiently.

1. Analyze Startup Costs and Potential Funding Options

Every business, no matter how small, comes with a **cost**. From registering your business to creating a website, paying for software, and sourcing materials or products, it's important to estimate your **startup costs** and understand how you'll fund these initial expenses.

Here's how to analyze your startup costs:

- **List all potential expenses:** Start by making a detailed list of everything you'll need to get started. These might include legal fees (like registering your business or obtaining licenses), technology costs (website hosting, domain registration, tools), marketing costs (advertising, graphic design), and product-related expenses (supplies, prototypes, shipping). Even small costs add up, so make sure you account for everything.

- **Estimate your monthly operational costs:** Once your business is running, there will be ongoing expenses. This could include subscription fees for software, inventory replenishment, office space, utilities, or employee wages (if applicable). It's important to know these numbers, so you can plan for them in advance.

- **Evaluate potential funding options:** Depending on the size and scope of your business, you may need some external funding to get started. Consider different options, such as:

  o **Bootstrapping:** Using your own savings or personal funds to finance your business. This is often the simplest approach but requires you to have enough savings to cover your startup costs.

  o **Loans:** Small business loans from banks or alternative lenders. Keep in mind that loans require repayment, so it's essential to ensure your business can generate enough cash flow to cover this.

- ○ **Crowdfunding:** Platforms like Kickstarter or Indiegogo can help you raise money from people who believe in your idea. This method also serves as a validation tool, as it proves people are willing to support your business upfront.

- ○ **Investors or Angel Funding:** If you're launching a scalable business with significant potential for growth, you might consider seeking investors. Angel investors or venture capitalists can provide funding in exchange for equity in your company.

By clearly understanding your **startup costs** and **funding options**, you can ensure that you're financially prepared to launch your business without overextending yourself.

2. Leverage Existing Skills and Tools

One of the most powerful resources at your disposal is your own **skill set.** When you leverage your existing expertise, you reduce the need to hire additional help or invest in expensive tools, especially in the early stages. Think about how you can make use of the skills and tools you already have to save both time and money.

Here's how to make the most of what you already know:

- **Identify transferable skills:** Reflect on your current job or past experiences to identify skills that could be applied to your business. For example, if you have experience in marketing, you can handle your own social media and content creation. If you're a writer, you can manage your blog and website copy.

- **Use free or low-cost tools:** There's no need to invest in expensive software or tools in the beginning. There are countless free or affordable platforms that can help you manage your business, such as:

    o **Website builders** like WordPress or Wix for creating a simple website.

- ○ **Canva** for graphic design and marketing materials.

- ○ **Trello** or **Asana** for task management.

- ○ **Mailchimp** for email marketing.

- ○ **Google Workspace** for document storage, communication, and scheduling.

- **Consider outsourcing selectively:** If there are skills you lack (for example, if you're not a designer or web developer), consider outsourcing specific tasks. Platforms like Upwork or Fiverr allow you to hire freelancers for one-time tasks at an affordable rate, rather than hiring full-time employees.

By using your existing skills and tools, you can **minimize startup costs** and avoid spending money on things that aren't essential to your business's initial launch.

3. Start with a Minimum Viable Product (MVP)

Instead of building a full-fledged product or service before you launch, consider starting with a **minimum viable product (MVP)**. An MVP is the simplest version of your product that solves the core problem for your target audience. It's focused on **testing** your business idea with real customers, gathering feedback, and then iterating based on that data.

Here's why starting with an MVP is crucial:

- **Validate your idea with less risk:** Rather than spending months and significant resources developing a fully-featured product, an MVP allows you to launch quickly and test your idea with real customers. This gives you valuable feedback before you make further investments.

- **Save time and money:** With an MVP, you focus only on the essential features that solve your target market's biggest problem. This allows you to get your business up and running with **minimal upfront costs** while still offering value to your customers.

- **Iterate based on feedback:** Once you launch your MVP, you can collect feedback from early users to improve your product. This ensures that you're building something people actually want, instead of investing heavily in a product that may not resonate with your market.

For example, if you're launching a new mobile app, instead of building every feature you envision, focus on one core feature that solves a problem. Once people start using it, you can add additional features based on their needs and requests.

Starting with an MVP allows you to take **small, manageable steps** and ensures that your idea is viable before you go all-in.

Aligning your business idea with your available resources—whether financial, skill-based, or time-related—helps you launch smarter and with less risk. By **assessing startup costs**, **leveraging your existing skills**, and focusing on an **MVP**, you'll ensure that your business is built on a solid foundation. This way, you can start small, test your concept, and scale up as resources allow.

Setting the Foundation for Success

We are moving quickly and as you can tell, things are starting to get a little more serious now. If you have not done so already, now is a great time to open a new document on your computer or grab a pen and paper (the old school way).

Define Your Business Mission and Goals

When you're starting a business, it's crucial to have a **clear sense of direction**. Defining your mission and setting specific goals helps you stay focused, measure progress, and align your actions with your long-term vision. This section will guide you through crafting a simple mission statement, setting clear and measurable objectives, and prioritizing your tasks for the first 20 days to get your business off the ground.

1. Craft a Simple Mission Statement

A **mission statement** is a concise declaration of your business's core purpose. It defines why your business exists, who you serve, and how you make a difference. A strong mission statement serves as a guiding light that keeps you and your team (if you have one) aligned on the bigger picture. It also helps your customers understand what your business stands for and what value it offers.

Here's how to craft a simple mission statement:

- **Identify your target audience:** Who are you serving? Be specific. Whether you're targeting busy parents, small business owners, or fitness enthusiasts, understanding your audience is the first step.

- **Clarify the problem you solve:** What problem does your business address? Make sure you articulate this clearly so it resonates with your audience. Think about the pain points your customers face and how your product or service can provide a solution.

- **Highlight your unique approach:** What makes your business different? This could be a unique feature, your approach to customer service, or the quality of your product. Distill this into a sentence or two that showcases how you stand out.

Example mission statement:

"We help busy professionals achieve work-life balance by providing simple, time-saving meal kits that are healthy, delicious, and easy to prepare."

This mission statement clearly defines the target audience (busy professionals), the problem being solved (work-life balance through meal prep), and the unique solution (simple, healthy, time-saving meal kits).

2. Set Clear, Measurable Objectives

While your mission statement gives you an overarching sense of purpose, your **objectives** are the concrete steps you need to take to achieve that mission. Setting **SMART goals** (Specific, Measurable, Achievable, Relevant, Time-bound) ensures that your objectives are actionable and trackable.

Here's how to set clear, measurable objectives for your business:

- **Be specific:** Vague goals like "I want to make money" or "I want to grow my business" are not helpful. Instead, define exactly what you want to achieve. For example, "I want to sell 100 units of my product in the next 30 days" is specific and measurable.

- **Break down larger goals into smaller steps:** Start with your big-picture goals (like growing your customer base or launching a product) and break them down into smaller, manageable objectives. For example, if your goal is to launch a product, your smaller steps might include designing the product, sourcing materials, building a website, and creating marketing content.

- **Use metrics to measure success:** For each objective, decide on a metric to measure success. For example:

    - **Customer acquisition:** "Gain 5o new followers on Instagram by the end of the month."

    - **Revenue goal:** "Generate $5oo in sales by the end of the first month."

    - **Product development:** "Complete product design and manufacturing by Day 15."

Setting measurable goals allows you to track progress and stay motivated as you check off milestones along the way.

3. Prioritize Tasks for the First 20 Days

Starting a business can feel overwhelming, but breaking your tasks down into **manageable chunks** is the key to staying focused and avoiding burnout. In the first 20 days, you'll want to prioritize the **most essential activities** that will lay the foundation for your business. Focus on actions that will either help you validate your idea, build your brand, or launch your product.

Here's how to prioritize tasks for the first 20 days:

- **Week 1: Establishing the Foundation**

  - Finalize your business name and mission statement.

  - Choose a business structure and register your business.

  - Set up a dedicated business email and phone number.

  - Begin researching your target audience and competitors.

- **Week 2: Building Your Presence**

  - Create a simple website or landing page.

- Set up social media profiles on key platforms (e.g., Instagram, Facebook, LinkedIn).

- Start creating content or messaging that resonates with your audience.

- Begin gathering feedback from potential customers (through surveys or informal interviews).

- **Week 3: Product/Service Development**

  - Finalize your product or service offering.

  - If applicable, create a minimum viable product (MVP) or prototype.

  - Set up an e-commerce platform (Shopify, Etsy, etc.) or create an order system.

  - Develop basic branding (logo, colors, and style).

- **Week 4: Launch Preparation**

  - Plan a launch strategy (social media posts, email campaigns, paid ads).

  - Set a soft launch date and start promoting your business.

- Create an introductory offer or incentive to encourage early customers.

- Prepare customer support or FAQs to handle inquiries.

By focusing on a clear set of priorities each week, you can make steady progress without feeling overwhelmed. Each of these tasks builds on the next, ensuring that your business is growing and moving toward launch.

Defining your **mission** and setting **clear, measurable goals** gives you direction and purpose, while **prioritizing tasks** ensures that you're spending your time and energy on what matters most. By focusing on these early steps, you create a strong foundation for your business and set yourself up for success in the long term.

Create a Productivity-Friendly Workspace

Whether you're launching your business from home, a shared office, or even a coffee shop, your workspace plays a huge role in determining how efficiently and effectively you work. By creating a **dedicated area** for work, keeping your **essential**

tools close by, and **minimizing distractions**, you can set yourself up to focus and make the most of your **10-minute-a-day business-building sessions**.

1. Choose a Dedicated Area for Work

Having a **designated space** for your business is essential to creating a boundary between work and personal life. Even if you're short on space, carving out a corner or a small nook can help you stay focused and productive.

Here's how to choose the best area:

- **Find a space with minimal foot traffic:** Look for a spot that's away from high-traffic areas in your home or office. This could be a quiet room, a corner of your living room, or even a spot at the local library. The key is to reduce the chances of being interrupted, especially if you're only working for short bursts of time.

- **Make it work-friendly:** If possible, choose a space that's ergonomically designed for work. Ensure your desk and chair are comfortable for sitting and that you have enough light to avoid eye strain. If you're working in a public space, use noise-canceling headphones or find a quiet corner where you can focus.

- **Keep it separate from relaxation areas:** If you work from home, keep your workspace separate from your relaxation zones (like your bed or couch). This helps you mentally separate "work mode" from "relaxation mode," making it easier to stay focused during your 10-minute sessions and switch off at the end of the day.

A dedicated, intentional workspace signals to your brain that it's time to work, even if you're only working for a few minutes a day. This is important especially if you have a busy house with kids, family or other distractions. Focus is key during your 10 minute sessions.

"Break down larger goals into smaller steps."

2. Keep Essential Tools Within Reach

When you're trying to make the most of your **10-minute business-building sessions**, the last thing you want is to waste time searching for tools, documents, or resources. To maximize efficiency, keep everything you need within arm's reach.

Here's how to organize your workspace for maximum productivity:

- **Set up your digital tools:** Ensure that your computer or laptop is set up with all the necessary software or tools you'll need, such as project management apps (Trello, Asana), communication tools (Slack, email), and design programs (Canva, Photoshop). If you rely on a physical calendar or planner, make sure it's visible and easy to reference.

- **Organize your physical space:** Keep your desk tidy and free from clutter. Only leave out the items that are essential for your work session. A clean, organized space helps reduce stress and distractions, making it easier to focus during your limited time. Consider using trays, organizers, or baskets to keep important documents, pens, and other supplies easily accessible.

- **Have backup tools ready:** In case something goes wrong (like technology failing or running out of supplies), have backup tools ready. For example, keep a notebook or pen handy if you need to jot down notes quickly, or have a backup charger and power bank for your devices.

The more streamlined your workspace, the more efficient your work sessions will be. Having everything you need within reach helps you **stay focused** and **avoid wasting precious time**.

3. Minimize Distractions in Your Environment

Distractions are one of the biggest barriers to productivity. To get the most out of your 10-minute-a-day sessions, it's essential to create an environment that minimizes interruptions and distractions.

Here's how to cut down on distractions:

- **Turn off notifications:** Whether it's social media, email, or other apps, notifications can pull your attention away from your work. Turn off non-essential notifications during your 10-minute work blocks, or use **Do Not Disturb** mode on your phone and computer.

- **Set boundaries with others:** If you work from home or share a workspace with others, set clear boundaries. Let family members, roommates, or colleagues know when you're in a focused work session and need uninterrupted time. If possible, use a sign or signal (like wearing headphones or closing your door) to indicate when you're in a work block.

- **Limit digital distractions:** If you find yourself distracted by websites or apps, consider using tools like **Freedom, Cold Turkey,** or **StayFocusd** to block distracting websites during your work sessions. These tools can help you stay on track and ensure you're not mindlessly scrolling when you should be focusing on your business.

- **Control your physical space:** Eliminate any clutter or objects that might tempt you to drift away from work. This includes toys, books, or even items that make you think of household chores. Keep your workspace minimalist and focused on business-related tasks.

By creating an environment that limits distractions, you can use your 10-minute sessions to make the most meaningful progress possible.

A productivity-friendly workspace doesn't have to be fancy, but it does need to be intentional. By **choosing a dedicated work area, keeping your essential tools handy,** and **minimizing distractions,** you set yourself up to work efficiently, even if you're only dedicating short bursts of time each day. The more you set your environment up for success, the easier it will be to stay focused and make consistent progress toward launching your business.

Prepare Mentally for the Journey

Starting a business is an exciting and rewarding journey, but it's also one that requires **mental resilience** and **focus.** Even with just 10 minutes a day, the path can sometimes feel overwhelming. That's why preparing yourself **mentally** is just as important as preparing your business plan. By scheduling reminders, practicing mindfulness, and visualizing your success, you can keep your mindset positive, calm, and motivated throughout the process.

1. Schedule Daily Reminders for Your Sessions

One of the biggest hurdles to consistency is simply **remembering** to take those 10 minutes each day. Life gets busy, and it's easy to let your business-building sessions slip through the cracks. The key to overcoming this is creating **daily reminders** that help you stay on track and integrate business tasks into your routine seamlessly.

Here's how to schedule reminders effectively:

- **Set recurring reminders:** Use your phone or digital calendar to set daily reminders for your business-building time. Make them recurring and set them at a time that works for you—whether that's in the morning, during a lunch break, or in the evening. These gentle nudges will keep you accountable and make it easier to

commit to your 10-minute work sessions
every day.

- **Create visual cues:** Place visual reminders
  in your environment—on your desk, your
  bathroom mirror, or your fridge. These
  can be simple notes like "10 minutes to
  business growth!" or "Take action now."
  The more you see these reminders, the
  more likely you are to take action,
  especially on days when motivation is low.

- **Use task management apps:** Tools like
  Trello, **Asana**, or **Todoist** can help you
  break your tasks into daily actions, keeping
  your to-do list clear and actionable. Many
  of these apps also offer reminder
  notifications to help keep you on track.

Scheduling reminders ensures that no matter how
busy your day gets, you don't forget to carve out
time for your business—and it makes those 10
minutes a regular habit in your routine.

2. Practice Mindfulness to Reduce Stress

Starting a business, even in small increments, can
be mentally taxing. It's easy to become
overwhelmed with the many moving parts of

entrepreneurship—especially if you're balancing a full-time job or family responsibilities. **Mindfulness** is an incredibly effective tool for reducing stress, improving focus, and keeping a clear head during this journey.

Here's how to integrate mindfulness into your business-building routine:

- **Start with deep breathing exercises:** Before diving into your 10-minute session, take a few moments to focus on your breath. Inhale deeply for a count of four, hold for four, and exhale slowly for a count of four. Doing this for 2-3 minutes can help calm your mind and reduce any tension or anxiety.

- **Practice present-moment awareness:** During your 10-minute work block, try to bring your full attention to the task at hand. If you feel your mind wandering or becoming stressed, gently bring it back to the present. Remind yourself that you're taking small steps each day, and that's all you need to focus on right now.

- **Take mindful breaks:** After your short work session, take a moment to pause and reflect. You might want to step away from your workspace for a few minutes, stretch, or walk around. This gives your mind a break and helps you reset before moving on to the next task.

Mindfulness allows you to **manage stress** effectively and stay focused, which is key to building momentum on your business journey without burning out.

3. Visualize Your Success Regularly

Visualization is a powerful mental technique that successful entrepreneurs use to stay motivated, focused, and positive. When you regularly visualize the **successful outcome** of your business, you're reinforcing a mindset of achievement and possibility. This can make the process feel less daunting and keep you inspired, even on tough days.

Here's how to practice visualization:

- **Picture your goals:** Close your eyes and imagine where you want your business to be in the next 3, 6, or 12 months. See yourself reaching milestones, whether it's hitting your first sale, launching your website, or gaining a loyal customer base. **The more vividly you imagine these successes,** the more real and achievable they will feel.

- **Visualize your process:** Don't just focus on the end result—also picture yourself going through the process. Visualize yourself working productively, overcoming obstacles, and staying consistent, even when things get difficult. This helps you feel more prepared and confident as you navigate the challenges that come with launching a business.

- **Use affirmations:** Alongside visualization, incorporate positive affirmations into your daily routine. Remind yourself that you are capable, strong, and on the path to success. Saying things like, "I am building my business one step at a time," can help reinforce a positive mindset and keep you motivated.

By regularly visualizing your success, you align your actions with your goals and cultivate a sense of **certainty** and **excitement** about the journey ahead.

Mentally preparing for your business journey is just as important as the physical work you put in. **Scheduling daily reminders,** practicing **mindfulness,** and **visualizing your success** can help you manage stress, stay focused, and maintain a positive mindset throughout your 10-minute-a-day sessions. With the right mental tools in place, you'll be more resilient, consistent, and motivated as you move closer to your goal of launching a successful business.

CHAPTER 2

Crafting a Solid Business Plan in Minutes

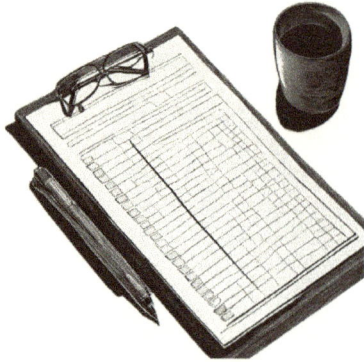

Drafting a Simplified Business Plan

Business plans can be quite complex at times. Let's remember a few key points to keep this going and maintain our momentum:

- ➤ this is a new business;

- ➤ we will likely need to pivot/adjust our plan;

- ➤ this is simply to guide us as we launch; and

> this must fit into the 10 minute a day strategy.

You can think of this business plan as the bumpers/railings they raise along the sides of a bowling lane when kids or inexperienced bowlers play. The rails ensure the ball stays on course, down the lane and reaches the end, sometimes bumping the sides along the way but never going into the gutter. I can tell you I am relieved when we put these guard rails/bumpers up with my kids!

Outline Your Business's Purpose

Before diving into the specifics, it's important to first understand why your business exists. A clear, simplified purpose acts as your guiding star—helping you stay focused on what matters most as you grow. Let's break this down into three easy steps.

1. Summarize Your Mission and Goals

Your mission is the foundation of your business. It's the "why" behind what you do, and it should resonate deeply with you and your customers. Don't overthink this—just articulate the core value you aim to provide. Keep it simple and straightforward. For example, if you're starting a business offering eco-friendly cleaning products, your mission might be: *"To help people create healthier, more sustainable homes with safe, green cleaning solutions."*

Once your mission is clear, identify a few goals that will guide you in achieving that mission. Focus on tangible, measurable goals, like *"Generate $2,000 in monthly revenue by the end of the first year"* or *"Sign up 100 subscribers for our email list in the first three months."* These goals give you direction and a sense of progress as you build your business.

2. Define Your Target Audience

Knowing who you're serving is just as important as knowing what you're offering. Your target audience is the group of people who will benefit most from your products or services. This isn't just about demographics—it's about understanding their needs, desires, and pain points.

Think about the problems your business solves and who is most affected by those problems. Are they busy parents? Entrepreneurs? Environmentally-conscious consumers? Be specific. The more clearly you define your audience, the easier it will be to create tailored marketing, products, and services that speak directly to them.

For instance, let's say you're launching a business that provides time-saving meal prep kits. Your target audience might be *"busy professionals aged 25-45 who want to eat healthier but struggle to find the time to cook."* The clearer your target audience, the sharper your messaging will be.

3. Identify Your Core Offerings

What exactly are you selling? Your core offerings should be the heart of your business. Whether it's a physical product, a digital service, or a combination of both, these are the things that your target audience needs or desires.

Focus on what sets your offerings apart from others in the market. Maybe it's the convenience of your product, the quality, or the unique way you deliver your service. Your offerings should solve a problem or enhance the life of your target audience in a meaningful way.

For example, if your mission is to help busy professionals eat healthier, your core offerings might include ready-to-prepare meal kits with organic ingredients, an easy-to-follow recipe guide, and delivery straight to their door. This is the backbone of your business and should align perfectly with both your mission and the needs of your audience.

Map Out Basic Financial Projections

Financial projections can feel overwhelming, but they don't need to be complicated. By mapping out a few basic numbers, you'll gain a clearer picture of what your business needs to get started and how you can begin generating revenue. This isn't about perfection—it's about giving yourself a framework to move forward with confidence.

1. Estimate Startup Costs

Before you dive into running your business, you need to know how much money it will take to get things off the ground. Your startup costs will depend on the nature of your business, but there are some common expenses you'll want to consider.

Think through the essentials, such as:

- **Legal fees:** Business registration, trademarks, contracts.

- **Technology and tools:** Website hosting, software subscriptions, payment processing.

- **Supplies and inventory:** Raw materials, packaging, or initial product stock.

- **Marketing and branding:** Logo design, promotional materials, initial advertising.

Keep in mind, you don't need to spend a fortune to launch. In fact, many businesses can be started with minimal upfront investment, especially in the digital age. Start small and scale as you go. The goal is to make a list of necessary expenses and come up with a rough estimate for each. This will give you a starting point to understand how much money you'll need in the early days.

For example, if you're starting a freelance writing business, your startup costs might be minimal—just a website domain, hosting, and perhaps some advertising to get your first clients. On the other hand, a retail business might require inventory, product samples, or even a small storefront. Be realistic, but don't get bogged down in trying to account for every possible expense. Just focus on the most important ones to launch.

2. Plan for Initial Revenue Streams

While costs are important, you also need to think about how you'll start making money. What will be your initial revenue streams? Are you offering a service, a physical product, or perhaps a subscription?

Map out how much you expect to earn in the first few months. Be realistic—don't assume you'll make six figures overnight (unless you have a proven formula). Start by thinking about smaller, achievable milestones. Maybe you aim to bring in $1,000 in your first month or sell 50 products.

Your revenue streams will also depend on your business model. If you're running a consulting business, your revenue might come from client retainers or project fees. If you're selling a product, your revenue might come from each sale. If your business involves recurring revenue, like a subscription service, factor in the expected number of subscribers over time.

For example, if you're launching an online course, you might project earning $500 from 10 students in the first month. This gives you a clear target and helps you keep track of progress. As you refine your marketing and sales strategies, you can adjust these projections over time.

3. Set a Realistic Budget for the First Month

Now that you have a sense of your startup costs and potential revenue, it's time to set a budget for your first month in business. This is your road map for how to spend your money wisely while keeping an eye on profitability.

Your first-month budget should include the essentials—everything you'll need to keep your business moving forward, including:

- **Marketing:** Online ads, social media promotion, or influencer outreach.

- **Product or service delivery:** Shipping, materials, tools, etc.

- **Operations:** Software, hosting fees, or any subscriptions necessary to run your business.

Remember, this first month is about testing, learning, and laying a solid foundation. Focus on spending where it matters most—on marketing that drives awareness, on tools that make your business run smoothly, and on the products or services you'll deliver to your customers.

To stay on track, break your budget into categories and set limits for each. If you're unsure of exactly what to spend, start with conservative estimates, and adjust as you go. For instance, you might allocate $200 for advertising, $100 for website hosting, and $300 for inventory.

Define a Clear Action Plan for Execution

A great idea and a solid plan are only as good as the execution behind them. In the early stages of launching your business, it's easy to feel like there's so much to do that you don't know where to start. But the key to overcoming that overwhelm is breaking everything down into small, manageable steps.

1. Break Down Tasks into Manageable Steps

The first step in creating an actionable plan is to identify everything you need to do—and then break those tasks down into smaller, bite-sized actions. It's easy to get caught up in grand to-do lists, but this process is about clarity.

For example, instead of writing "Create website," break it down into smaller tasks like:

- Choose a domain name.

- Register the domain.

- Pick a website platform (e.g., WordPress, Shopify).

- Design homepage layout.

- Write "About Us" section.

- Select products or services to feature.

- Set up payment processing.

This makes your overall goal feel less daunting because you're focusing on one small thing at a time. Plus, every time you complete one of these smaller tasks, you'll build momentum, making the next task easier.

2. Assign Time Frames to Each Step

Once you've broken down your tasks, it's time to assign a realistic time frame to each one. Be mindful of your busy schedule, and give yourself enough time to complete each task without feeling rushed.

For example, if "Pick a website platform" is one of your tasks, set a time frame like "15 minutes today to review three website platforms." Setting time limits will help you stay focused and avoid perfectionism that can keep you from moving forward. The key is to make consistent progress, not necessarily to do everything perfectly.

When assigning time frames, start with the assumption that you'll only be working for 10 minutes at a time. This allows for flexibility and accommodates your busy life. For larger tasks, you might want to break them into smaller chunks that can each be completed in a short amount of time. Just remember—every little step you take is progress.

3. Focus on Milestones Achievable in 10 Minutes

Now comes the most important part: focus on milestones that you can achieve in just 10 minutes. If you commit to taking action every single day—even if it's just for 10 minutes—you'll be amazed at how quickly you'll move forward.

A 10-minute action plan might look like this:

- **Day 1:** Spend 10 minutes brainstorming possible domain names.

- **Day 2:** Use 10 minutes to research three competitors in your niche.

- **Day 3:** Write 10 minutes' worth of copy for your website's homepage.

- **Day 4:** Spend 10 minutes drafting your social media marketing plan.

In just a few days, you'll find that these tiny bursts of effort add up to real progress. And because they're short, it's easier to stay motivated. This consistent, incremental approach ensures that you're not trying to juggle a hundred tasks at once, and it keeps your stress levels low. Small wins lead to bigger wins.

Remember, the goal is not to finish everything in one day or one week but to start building momentum with focused action. If you keep showing up, even in small bursts, you'll begin to see how quickly you can turn your vision into reality—one 10-minute session at a time.

Researching Your Market

Identify Your Target Audience

Understanding your target audience is crucial for tailoring your business to the people who need it most. To truly connect with potential customers, you must dig deep into who they are, what they care about, and how they make purchasing decisions. When you have a clear picture of your audience, you'll be able to craft offerings that resonate and develop marketing strategies that speak directly to their needs.

1. Define Demographics and Psychographics

The first step in identifying your target audience is breaking them down into demographics and psychographics.

- **Demographics** are the basic statistical characteristics of your audience. This includes factors like:
  - **Age:** Are you targeting young adults, middle-aged professionals, or retirees?

- **Gender:** Does your business cater to a specific gender or is it gender-neutral?

- **Location:** Are your customers local, national, or international? Do you want to target urban areas or rural communities?

- **Income level:** What is your audience's average income? Are they budget-conscious or willing to spend more for premium offerings?

- **Occupation:** What kinds of jobs do your potential customers have? Are they entrepreneurs, busy professionals, stay-at-home parents?

- **Psychographics** go deeper into understanding the values, interests, and lifestyles of your audience. These include:

  - **Values:** What do they care about? Is sustainability important to them? Do they value quality or convenience above all?

- **Hobbies and interests:** What do they enjoy doing in their free time? Do they follow specific trends or communities?

- **Lifestyle:** Are they health-conscious, career-driven, or family-focused? Are they risk-takers or prefer stability?

Together, demographics and psychographics give you a well-rounded profile of your target audience. For example, if you're selling fitness equipment, you might target women aged 25-40 who are health-conscious, active, and value high-quality, eco-friendly products.

2. Research Audience Pain Points

To truly serve your target audience, you need to understand the problems they face. What keeps them up at night? What are their frustrations or struggles? These pain points will be the driving force behind their purchasing decisions.

Start by asking yourself:

- **What problem does my product or service solve?**

- **What challenges are my potential customers trying to overcome?**

- **What do they need that they can't easily get elsewhere?**

For example, if you're offering a time management app, the pain point for your audience could be that they feel overwhelmed by their busy schedules and lack of organization. By addressing this pain point, your marketing and product development will resonate with your audience in a meaningful way.

To gather insights, consider:

- **Talking to your audience:** Use surveys, social media, or direct conversations to ask your current or potential customers about their challenges.

- **Researching online:** Read reviews of similar products or services. What are people complaining about? What do they wish they had in a product?

- **Looking at industry trends:** Is there a growing need or concern in your industry that you can solve?

When you fully understand your audience's pain points, you'll be in a much better position to design a solution that feels tailor-made for them.

3. Analyze Purchasing Habits

Next, it's important to understand how your audience makes purchasing decisions. People don't just buy products because they need them— they buy based on a range of factors, including timing, convenience, and emotions.

- **Where do they shop?** Do they prefer online shopping or do they like to visit brick-and-mortar stores? Are they impulse buyers or do they carefully research before purchasing?

- **How do they pay?** Are they likely to use credit cards, mobile payments, or cash? Do they expect discounts or special offers before committing?

- **What influences their decision?** Do they value product reviews, word-of-mouth recommendations, or influencer endorsements? Are they motivated by social proof, a sense of urgency, or special deals?

For instance, if you're selling high-end skincare, you might find that your target audience prefers to shop online, values product reviews, and is willing to pay a premium for trusted brands. This knowledge will guide your pricing strategy, your marketing approach, and your sales tactics.

Look at your competitors: What strategies are they using to target the same audience? What can you do differently, or better? This will help you refine your own approach and ensure you're aligning your offerings with your audience's purchasing behaviors.

"Commit to taking action every single day."

Study Your Competitors

In the world of business, you're never truly working in a vacuum. No matter what industry you're in, there are always others offering similar products or services. Studying your competitors will give you a strategic advantage, helping you understand what's already working in the market, where the gaps are, and how you can position your business to stand out. It's not about copying others—it's about learning from them and carving out your own unique space.

1. Identify Direct and Indirect Competitors

The first step in studying your competitors is identifying who they are. Competitors come in two forms: **direct** and **indirect**.

- **Direct competitors** are businesses that offer the same or very similar products or services to the same target audience. If you're opening a coffee shop in your neighborhood, other coffee shops nearby are your direct competitors. Their offerings, pricing, and marketing strategies will give you a good sense of what you're up against.

- **Indirect competitors**, on the other hand, are businesses that meet the same needs or solve similar problems but do it in a different way. If you're selling healthy snacks, for example, your direct competitors are other snack companies, but your indirect competitors could be meal delivery services or even local farmers' markets. They may not be doing exactly what you do, but they're providing an alternative solution to the same customer need.

Make a list of both direct and indirect competitors in your niche. Understanding the full landscape—both direct and indirect—will help you assess where there's room for you to fit in and thrive.

2. Compare Pricing and Offerings

Once you've identified your competitors, the next step is to compare what they offer and how much they charge. This will give you insights into the market rate and help you position your pricing competitively. Here's how you can do this:

- **Pricing:** Are your competitors premium brands with high prices, or do they offer budget-friendly options? What is the price range for the core products or services they offer?

- **Product or Service Features:** What exactly are they selling? What features or benefits do their products or services include? Are they focusing on quality, convenience, or innovation?

- **Customer Experience:** How is the experience they provide? Is it easy for customers to browse, purchase, and receive support? What's their return policy? Do they offer fast shipping or flexible payment plans?

By evaluating pricing and offerings, you'll get a better sense of how you can structure your own products and pricing. Are you aiming to be a low-cost provider? Or do you want to offer premium services with added value? This comparison helps you decide on your own approach to both pricing and service.

For instance, if your direct competitors offer basic products at a lower price point, you might decide to differentiate yourself by offering more premium features, better customer service, or additional benefits (like a loyalty program or exclusive content).

3. Note Unique Selling Points (USPs)

Your Unique Selling Proposition (USP) is what sets you apart from everyone else in the market. It's the one thing that makes your business special. By studying your competitors, you can pinpoint what they're doing well—and where they're falling short—so you can carve out your own unique position.

To uncover the USPs of your competitors, ask yourself:

- **What do they do better than anyone else?** Are they known for their fast delivery? Their exceptional customer service? Their unique product features?

- **What's missing?** What gaps can you fill that others aren't addressing? Maybe your competitors offer great products, but their customer service is lacking. Or maybe they have a strong brand, but their pricing doesn't fit your target market.

By understanding what's already out there, you can clearly define your own USP. Your USP could be anything from offering a wider variety of options, to solving a specific pain point in a unique way, to providing unmatched quality or customer experience. Whatever it is, make sure it's something that resonates with your target audience and makes you stand out.

For example, if your competitors offer high-quality organic food but don't focus on sustainability in their packaging, you might position your business as the eco-friendly alternative—selling organic food in 100% recyclable or compostable packaging.

Position Your Business for Success

Positioning your business for success isn't just about offering a good product or service—it's about ensuring that your brand stands out in a crowded marketplace and resonates deeply with your target audience. It's about crafting a compelling story that tells customers why they should choose you over your competitors, and then delivering on that promise every single time. Here's how you can do it.

1. Craft a Unique Value Proposition (UVP)

Your **Unique Value Proposition** (UVP) is the heart of your business positioning. It's the clear statement that tells your customers why your product or service is the best solution to their problem. Your UVP should be simple, direct, and focused on the key benefits that set you apart from competitors.

Ask yourself:

- What problem am I solving for my customers?

- What makes my solution better or different from others?

- Why should customers choose my business over anyone else?

Your UVP should be a concise statement that highlights the **specific value** you provide in a way that resonates with your audience's needs. For example:

- *"We help busy professionals eat healthier by delivering fresh, pre-portioned meals directly to their door, so they can save time and eat well without the stress."*

- *"Our eco-friendly cleaning products are safe for your home and the planet, offering a powerful clean without harsh chemicals."*

The key is to make sure that your UVP addresses a key pain point and clearly communicates the unique benefits of your offering. Your UVP should be the core message that guides all of your marketing efforts.

2. Highlight Your Competitive Advantages

Once you've defined your UVP, you need to focus on the specific **competitive advantages** that make your business the best choice. These are the factors that give you an edge over other businesses in your space.

Your competitive advantages could be based on:

- **Product features:** Do you offer superior quality, unique functionality, or innovative designs that competitors lack?

- **Customer experience:** Are you known for providing exceptional service, fast response times, or a more personalized approach?

- **Price point:** Are you offering better value at a more affordable price, or are you positioned as a premium brand offering exclusive features?

- **Convenience:** Are your products or services easier to access, more flexible, or faster than what's available elsewhere?

For example, if you run a clothing store that specializes in custom-fit apparel, your competitive advantage could be the ability to offer perfectly tailored clothes at an affordable price. If you're running an online business, it might be your lightning-fast shipping or your unmatched customer support.

Identifying and emphasizing your competitive advantages helps build credibility and trust with your audience. It shows potential customers why they should choose you over anyone else.

3. Focus on Delivering Exceptional Value

While positioning your business is important, **delivering exceptional value** is what will keep your customers coming back for more. Your business isn't just about selling products or services; it's about creating an experience that leaves your customers feeling like they got more than what they expected.

To deliver exceptional value, focus on:

- **Quality:** Always ensure that your product or service meets or exceeds customer expectations. Whether it's the durability of your product or the thoroughness of your customer service, quality should be non-negotiable.

- **Customer experience:** Make every touchpoint with your business memorable.

From your website design to how you answer the phone to how your product is packaged—every detail counts.

- **Ongoing support:** Offer excellent post-purchase support. If your customers have a question or problem, be ready to assist them quickly and efficiently.

- **Consistency:** Ensure that your business delivers the same high level of value every time. Whether it's the same experience online or in person, consistency builds trust and loyalty.

For instance, if you're offering a subscription-based service, ensuring timely deliveries, easy returns, and a hassle-free experience will create exceptional value. It's about making your customers feel confident and valued at every stage of their journey with your business.

Organizing Your Business Structure

Choose a Legal Structure

Choosing the right legal structure for your business is one of the most important decisions you'll make. Your choice will impact everything from your personal liability to your tax responsibilities, and it can even affect your ability to raise capital or hire employees. While this might sound like a daunting decision, don't worry—let's break it down into clear, manageable steps so you can confidently choose the best option for your business.

1. Compare Sole Proprietorship, LLC, and Corporation Options

The three most common legal structures for small businesses are **sole proprietorships**, **Limited Liability Companies (LLCs)**, and **corporations**. Each has its own advantages and disadvantages, so let's compare them based on key factors like liability, taxes, and ease of setup.

- **Sole Proprietorship:**
  A sole proprietorship is the simplest and most common business structure. If you're the only owner, your business is automatically a sole proprietorship unless you choose a different structure.

  - **Pros:**

- Easiest and least expensive to set up.

- You have complete control over decision-making.

- Taxes are straightforward—profits and losses are reported on your personal tax return.

  ○ **Cons:**

- Personal liability: As a sole proprietor, you are personally responsible for all debts, obligations, and legal actions related to your business. This means your personal assets could be at risk if things go wrong.

- **LLC (Limited Liability Company):**
An LLC is a more formal structure that combines the simplicity of a sole proprietorship with the liability protection of a corporation.

  ○ **Pros:**

- Limited liability: Your personal assets are protected from business debts and lawsuits.

- Flexible tax options: You can choose to be taxed as a sole proprietor, partnership, S corporation, or C corporation, depending on your goals.

- Less paperwork and administrative requirements than a corporation.

  ○ **Cons:**

    - More complex and costly to set up than a sole proprietorship.

    - May require annual fees or reports, depending on your state.

- **Corporation (C Corporation or S Corporation):**
  Corporations are separate legal entities from their owners (shareholders). While

there are both **C corporations** and **S corporations**, the distinction mostly comes down to how they're taxed.

- Pros:
    - Limited liability: Shareholders' personal assets are protected from business debts and liabilities.
    - Ability to raise capital through stock issuance.
    - Potential tax advantages with an S Corporation (such as avoiding double taxation).
- Cons:
    - More complex and expensive to set up and maintain.
    - Double taxation for C Corporations: The company pays taxes on profits, and then shareholders pay taxes on dividends received.

- Corporate formalities and more paperwork (annual meetings, minutes, etc.).

2. Consider Legal and Tax Implications

Your choice of legal structure will impact both your **liability** and your **taxes**. Here's a breakdown of these important considerations:

- **Liability Protection:**
    - **Sole proprietorships** offer no personal liability protection, which means that if your business gets into financial trouble or is sued, you could be personally liable.
    - **LLCs** offer protection, meaning your personal assets (like your home or savings) are shielded from business liabilities.
    - **Corporations** provide the strongest protection, separating you entirely from your business entity.

- **Taxation:**
    - **Sole proprietorships** have **pass-through taxation,** meaning that

business profits and losses are reported on your personal income tax return. This can be advantageous for tax simplicity but could lead to higher taxes if your business grows large.

○ **LLCs** offer **pass-through taxation** as well, but you can also elect to be taxed as a corporation if it benefits your business. For example, if you want to avoid self-employment taxes, electing S Corporation status can be beneficial.

○ **Corporations** are subject to **double taxation** (in the case of a C Corporation), meaning the business is taxed on its profits, and then shareholders are taxed again when they receive dividends. However, if you choose S Corporation status, you can avoid double taxation, as income is passed through to shareholders' personal tax returns.

3. Research Requirements for Your Region

The requirements for each legal structure can vary depending on where you live. Each state or country has its own rules, fees, and paperwork, so it's important to do your homework. Here are a few things to consider:

- **State-specific regulations:** Some states may have different rules for LLCs or corporations, such as annual fees, franchise taxes, or mandatory filings. For example, states like Delaware and Nevada are popular for incorporating due to favorable business laws, while other states may be more stringent.

- **Permits and licenses:** Depending on your business type and location, you may need specific licenses or permits to operate legally. For example, a food-related business will need health permits, while a home-based business might need zoning approval.

- **Ongoing requirements:** Consider any ongoing compliance tasks required for your chosen structure. For LLCs and corporations, there may be annual reporting, taxes, or franchise fees, depending on your region.

Bonus Tip: Consult with a local business attorney or accountant to ensure you're selecting the best structure for your business goals and complying with all local laws and tax regulations.

Register Your Business

Once you've chosen your business structure, the next step is to officially register your business. This process will make your business a legal entity and ensure you're compliant with local, state, and federal regulations. Registering your business is also essential for building credibility and protecting your brand. Let's break down the key steps to getting your business properly registered.

1. Check the Availability of Your Business Name

Before you start printing business cards or building your website, you need to make sure that the name you've chosen is available and legally protected. Here's what you need to do:

- **Search online databases:** Start by searching your state's business registry and the U.S. Patent and Trademark Office (USPTO) database to ensure that the name isn't already in use. You can also check if there's a domain name available for your website.

- **Consider trademarking your name:** If you're planning to grow your business long-term, it's worth considering trademarking your business name. A trademark helps protect your name and logo from being used by others in your industry. It's an extra layer of protection that ensures your brand identity remains unique.

- **Domain name availability:** It's also a good idea to check if the domain name for your business is available. Ideally, you'll want your website URL to match your business name. Tools like GoDaddy or Namecheap can help you quickly check domain name availability.

2. Follow State or Local Registration Processes

Once you've confirmed your business name is available, it's time to officially register your business with the relevant state or local authorities. The process will depend on your business structure and location. Here are the general steps:

- **Registering a sole proprietorship:** In many cases, you don't need to register a sole proprietorship with the state, but you may need to file a "Doing Business As" (DBA) or trade name registration. This lets your state or county know that you're operating under a name other than your own.

- **Registering an LLC or Corporation:** If you've chosen an LLC or Corporation, you'll need to file articles of organization (for LLCs) or articles of incorporation (for corporations) with your state. This is typically done through the Secretary of State's office or a similar state agency.

   - For an LLC, you'll also need to pay a filing fee, which varies by state.

   - For corporations, you may also need to establish a board of directors and hold an initial meeting.

- **Get an Employer Identification Number (EIN):** Regardless of your business structure, you'll likely need to obtain an EIN from the IRS. This number is like a Social Security number for your business and is required for tax purposes, opening a business bank account, and hiring employees. You can apply for an EIN for free through the IRS website.

- **Register with the local government:** In some areas, you may need to register your business with the local county or city government as well. This is particularly important for businesses that operate in certain industries (like retail or food services) or are based in specific areas. Check with your local city hall or county office to ensure you're following all necessary local requirements.

3. Obtain Any Necessary Permits or Licenses

Depending on the type of business you're starting and your location, you may need specific permits or licenses to legally operate. These vary by industry and jurisdiction, but here's a general overview of what you might need:

- **Federal licenses or permits:** Some businesses, such as those involved in agriculture, alcohol, or firearms, require a federal license or permit. You can check the U.S. Small Business Administration (SBA) website to see if your business falls under federal regulations.

- **State licenses or permits:** Many businesses need state-level permits or licenses. For example, a cosmetology business may need a state-issued cosmetology license, while a contractor might need a state contractor's license. Check your state's business website to see which licenses apply to your specific business type.

- **Local permits or licenses:** In addition to state and federal requirements, your local government may require a business license to operate. Cities or counties often require businesses to register, especially if you're operating a physical storefront or offering certain services. This can include health permits, signage permits, and more.

- **Industry-specific licenses:** Depending on your industry, you may need specialized permits. For example:

  ○ Food-related businesses need health and safety permits.

  ○ Home-based businesses may need zoning approval to ensure you can legally operate from your residence.

  ○ If you're in construction, you may need contractor-specific permits or bonding.

Be sure to consult with your local chamber of commerce or industry associations to determine exactly what permits or licenses you need. Applying for these permits early in the process will help you avoid delays or fines down the road.

Open a Dedicated Business Account

One of the most important steps in launching your business is separating your personal and business finances. A dedicated business account will help you keep your finances organized, maintain legal protection, and avoid complications come tax time. It also adds a layer of professionalism to your business operations. Here's how to set yourself up for financial success right from the start.

1. Choose a Reliable Bank for Your Needs

Selecting the right bank for your business is crucial, as it will serve as the foundation for all your financial transactions. When choosing a bank, consider the following:

- **Business-specific accounts:** Make sure the bank offers business accounts tailored to your needs. Look for checking accounts that allow for easy deposits, transfers, and access to your funds. Many banks also offer specialized accounts for small businesses that include features like free business checks, low monthly fees, and access to business credit.

- **Convenience and accessibility:** Consider a bank that has branches near you or offers convenient online banking services, so you can easily manage your account on-the-go. Also, check whether the bank offers mobile check deposits, which can be a huge time-saver.

- **Fees and charges:** Compare fees and charges across different banks. Some banks offer free business accounts with no monthly maintenance fees, while others may charge for account maintenance, ATM usage, or excess transactions. Make sure to choose an option that fits your budget and business activity.

- **Additional services:** Look for a bank that provides additional services such as credit cards, loans, and lines of credit that could be useful as your business grows. Access to small business loans or financing can be particularly valuable if you plan to scale your business in the future.

2. Separate Personal and Business Finances

One of the key reasons to open a dedicated business account is to keep your **personal and business finances separate.** Mixing the two can lead to confusion, make it difficult to track your profits and expenses, and potentially cause problems when filing taxes or applying for business loans. Here's how to do it:

- **Use the business account for all business transactions:** From day one, make it a rule to use your business account for all business-related expenses and income. This includes payments for supplies, employee wages, invoices from clients, and any other operational costs.

- **Keep personal expenses out of your business account:** Avoid transferring personal funds into your business account or using business funds for personal purchases. Mixing finances can complicate bookkeeping and can cause legal or tax issues down the road, especially if your business is set up as an LLC or corporation.

- **Track everything accurately:** Having a separate account makes it easier to track business transactions for tax purposes. Plus, it can help you see your business's cash flow more clearly, making it easier to make informed decisions.

By keeping personal and business finances separate, you ensure a cleaner, more professional approach to managing money, and reduce the risk of accidental mistakes or oversights.

3. Explore Tools for Tracking Income and Expenses

Tracking your income and expenses is essential for keeping your business financially healthy. The good news is, there are plenty of **tools and software** available to make this process easier.

- **Accounting software:** Tools like **QuickBooks**, **Xero**, and **Wave** can automatically sync with your bank account and categorize your transactions, making it easy to track income, expenses, and profit margins. These tools also generate reports to help you understand your financial health, and some even let you send invoices or pay bills directly from the platform.

- **Expense tracking apps:** If you prefer a simpler system, apps like **Expensify** or **Shoeboxed** can help you track expenses on the go by scanning receipts and categorizing your spending. These tools also allow you to create reports, which can be incredibly useful for tax preparation.

- **Spreadsheets:** If you're just getting started and prefer a DIY approach, simple spreadsheets (such as Google Sheets or Excel) can be an effective tool to track income and expenses. You can create columns for income, expenses, and profits, and easily update the spreadsheet regularly.

- **Mobile banking apps:** Many banks now offer mobile apps with expense tracking features that can automatically categorize and track transactions. These apps often sync with your business bank account, giving you real-time updates on your financial activity.

Regardless of the tool you choose, the key is consistency. Set aside time regularly—ideally weekly or monthly—to update your records, review your transactions, and ensure everything is in order. By staying organized, you'll not only be prepared for tax time but also gain valuable insights into the financial performance of your business.

CHAPTER 3

Building and Marketing Your Business

Establishing Your Brand

Keeping in mind we want to keep this moving along with reasonable to no costs, this is an excellent opportunity to include family or friends to help with the art work for the logo and any associated branding package. Perhaps you have kids who are gifted artists, maybe your significant other has a keen eye for style and images. This is the time to get them involved, they will appreciate knowing what you;ve been sneaking away doing for 10 minute a night!

Design a Compelling Logo and Branding Elements

Your business's **branding** is more than just a logo—it's the visual identity that communicates who you are, what you do, and the value you offer. Whether you're selling a product or providing a service, strong branding helps you stand out, build trust with your audience, and make a lasting impression. In this section, we'll walk through how to **choose the right colors and fonts, use online tools for quick logo creation**, and **keep your branding consistent** across platforms to create a professional and compelling brand identity.

1. Choose Colors and Fonts That Resonate with Your Audience

The right colors and fonts can evoke emotions, convey your brand's personality, and influence how people perceive your business. When designing your branding, it's important to choose colors and fonts that align with your **business goals** and **target audience**.

Here's how to make these choices:

- **Colors:**
  Colors are powerful psychological tools. Different colors evoke different emotions and can influence how your audience connects with your brand. For example:

  - **Blue** conveys trust and professionalism.

  - **Red** is associated with energy, passion, and urgency.

  - **Green** often represents health, nature, and growth.

  - **Yellow** symbolizes optimism and friendliness.

- To find the right colors for your business, think about what emotions you want to elicit from your customers. If you're in the health and wellness space, calm colors like blue or green might work well. If you're in the fitness industry, bold colors like red or orange might be more appropriate. Stick to **two or three primary colors** to maintain a clean, cohesive look.

- **Fonts:**

  Like colors, fonts convey personality.
  Choose fonts that are **legible** and reflect
  your brand's tone. For example:

  - **Serif fonts** (like Times New Roman)
    are formal and traditional.

  - **Sans-serif fonts** (like Helvetica) are
    modern and sleek.

  - **Script fonts** (like Pacifico) are more
    personal and elegant.

- Limit the number of fonts you use to **two
  or three**—one for headings, one for body
  text, and one for accents (if necessary).
  This ensures your branding remains clean
  and easy to read, whether on your website,
  social media, or promotional materials.

2. Use Online Tools for Quick Logo Creation

Designing a logo from scratch can feel like a
daunting task, but luckily, there are many **online
tools** that allow you to create a logo quickly and
affordably—even if you don't have design
experience. These tools provide templates, icons,
and customization options that allow you to

create a **professional-looking logo** in just a few minutes.

Here are some great options for quick logo creation:

- **Canva:** Canva offers a vast collection of logo templates that you can customize to suit your business. You can adjust colors, fonts, and icons easily, even if you have zero design skills. Canva's free version is robust, and their paid version unlocks even more features.

- **Looka:** Looka uses AI to generate logo designs based on your preferences. By inputting your business name, industry, and style preferences, Looka will create several logo options, which you can tweak further. You can download your logo and brand kit once you're happy with the design.

- **Hatchful by Shopify:** Hatchful is a free tool from Shopify that helps you design logos quickly by selecting a template and customizing it with your colors, fonts, and icons. It's user-friendly and offers templates for various industries.

- **LogoMaker:** LogoMaker allows you to create a logo in minutes with a simple step-by-step process. You can explore hundreds of design options and download your finished logo after making your customizations.

When using these tools, keep your **brand identity** in mind. Your logo should represent your mission, values, and the unique aspects of your business. After you create a logo, **download it in different file formats** (e.g., PNG, SVG, JPEG) to ensure it's ready for all types of use.

3. Keep Branding Consistent Across Platforms

Once you've developed your logo and chosen your color palette and fonts, the next step is to ensure that your branding is **consistent** across all platforms. Whether it's your website, social media, or marketing materials, having a cohesive look and feel is crucial for building brand recognition and trust with your audience.

Here's how to maintain consistency:

- **Use the same color palette everywhere:** Whether on your website, social media profiles, or printed materials, make sure your colors are consistent. Stick to your primary and secondary colors across all touchpoints, so customers can immediately recognize your brand.

- **Standardize fonts:** Use the same fonts for headers, body text, and other elements across your website, social media posts, and marketing materials. This ensures your messaging feels cohesive and professional. Some website builders like **WordPress** and **Wix** allow you to upload custom fonts for easy consistency.

- **Logo placement and sizing:** Make sure your logo is placed consistently across all platforms. On social media, for example, use your logo as your profile picture, and make sure it fits well in the available space (without being stretched or cropped). Similarly, ensure the logo's size remains consistent on your website and promotional materials.

- **Create a brand style guide:** If you plan to expand your team or work with freelancers (like designers, copywriters, or marketers), having a **brand style guide** ensures that everyone uses the same colors, fonts, and logo placement guidelines. A style guide doesn't have to be complicated—it can simply include your brand's colors, fonts, logo usage, and any specific visual elements you want to include.

Consistency is key when it comes to building a recognizable and trustworthy brand. By keeping your branding elements aligned across platforms, your business will feel more cohesive and professional, helping you make a lasting impression on your audience.

Designing a compelling logo and establishing consistent branding is a crucial step in creating a strong, recognizable identity for your business. By **choosing colors and fonts** that resonate with your audience, using **online tools** for quick logo creation, and maintaining **branding consistency**, you'll build a professional image that attracts customers and fosters trust from day one.

Create a Simple but Professional Website

In today's digital world, a **professional website** is essential for building credibility and attracting customers. Whether you're offering a product, service, or information, your website acts as the digital storefront for your business. It doesn't need to be complicated, but it should **reflect your brand**, showcase your **key offerings**, and make it easy for visitors to contact you. This section will guide you through how to create a simple, yet professional website that gets results.

1. Choose an Easy-to-Use Website Builder

When starting out, it's crucial to choose a website builder that's intuitive and doesn't require any coding knowledge. Luckily, there are many platforms designed for beginners that allow you to create a website quickly and easily without sacrificing professionalism.

Here are some great website builders to consider:

- **Wix:** Wix is known for its drag-and-drop editor, making it extremely easy to design your website. With plenty of templates to choose from, you can quickly create a professional-looking site. They also offer various pricing plans, including free options with some limitations.

- **Squarespace:** Squarespace offers sleek, modern templates ideal for those looking for a professional design with minimal effort. It's particularly great for creative businesses, bloggers, and e-commerce shops. Their pricing includes hosting and a free domain for the first year.

- **WordPress.com:** WordPress is a popular choice, offering flexibility with its themes and plugins. It's a bit more advanced than Wix or Squarespace but still beginner-friendly. WordPress.com also offers a free version, though paid plans unlock more features and customization options.

- **Shopify:** If you're launching an e-commerce business, Shopify is one of the best platforms for creating an online store. It's designed to help you sell products, manage inventory, and process payments, all in one place.

When choosing a website builder, consider the specific needs of your business. If you plan to sell products, opt for an e-commerce-focused platform like **Shopify** or **Squarespace**. If you just need a simple informational site, **Wix** or **WordPress** might be more suitable.

2. Highlight Key Offerings and Contact Information

Your website should quickly convey who you are, what you offer, and how visitors can get in touch with you. **Keep it simple, clean, and focused**—highlight the most important information, so visitors don't get overwhelmed or confused.

Here's how to structure your site:

- **Homepage:** The homepage should immediately tell visitors what your business does and who you serve. This can be done through a concise headline or tagline that clearly explains your value proposition. Include a brief description of your business and call-to-action buttons (like "Learn More" or "Get Started") to guide visitors to the next step.

- **Key Offerings (Products or Services):** Create a dedicated page or section that outlines your main products or services. Use clear headings, short descriptions, and high-quality images to explain what you're offering. Focus on the **benefits** your offerings provide, not just the features. For example, instead of just saying "10% off all orders," you could write, "Save 10% on your first order—perfect for trying out our product!"

- **Contact Information:** Make it easy for visitors to get in touch with you. Include a contact page with your email address, phone number (if applicable), and possibly a contact form for inquiries. You can also add links to your social media profiles so visitors can engage with you across multiple platforms.

- **Clear Navigation:** Your website's navigation should be intuitive and easy to follow. Make sure your main pages (like Home, About, Services, Contact) are easy to find, and limit the number of pages to keep things streamlined.

"Keep branding consistent."

3. Optimize for Mobile Users

With more people accessing the internet from their phones than ever before, **mobile optimization** is no longer optional—it's essential.

A website that looks great on desktop but doesn't work well on mobile can turn potential customers away.

Here's how to ensure your website is mobile-friendly:

- **Responsive Design:** Most modern website builders (like Wix, Squarespace, and WordPress) offer responsive templates, meaning they'll automatically adjust to look good on mobile devices. Before publishing your site, preview it on a mobile device to ensure everything looks great and functions properly.

- **Simple Layout:** Mobile screens are smaller, so it's important to keep your design **clean and simple.** Use large fonts for easy readability, and make buttons large enough to click without zooming in. Avoid cluttering your pages with too much text or too many images.

- **Fast Loading Speed:** Mobile users are often on the go and may not have fast internet connections. Ensure your website loads quickly by compressing large images, removing unnecessary plugins, and using a reliable hosting provider. Tools like **Google PageSpeed Insights** can help you analyze your site's speed and identify areas for improvement.

- **Easy Navigation on Mobile:** On mobile devices, your navigation menu should be easy to use with one hand. Use a **hamburger menu** (three lines stacked together) for your navigation links, and make sure buttons are spaced out enough to avoid accidental clicks.

Creating a simple yet professional website doesn't need to be an overwhelming task. By **choosing an easy-to-use website builder**, **highlighting key offerings and contact information**, and **optimizing for mobile users**, you can create a site that not only looks great but also converts visitors into customers. With just a few straightforward steps, you'll have a digital presence that showcases your brand and helps you achieve your business goals.

Establish Your Social Media Presence

In today's business landscape, social media is one of the most powerful tools you can use to build your brand, connect with potential customers, and drive traffic to your website. However, with so many platforms available, it's essential to **focus on the ones most relevant to your audience**. This section will guide you through how to select the best social media platforms, set up professional profiles, and plan an initial content strategy that helps you grow your presence online.

1. Select Platforms Most Relevant to Your Audience

There's no one-size-fits-all answer when it comes to social media, so it's important to focus your efforts on the platforms where your target audience is most active. Think about your **ideal customer's demographics**—age, gender, location, interests—and where they're likely to spend their time online.

Here are some of the most popular platforms and what types of businesses and audiences they attract:

- **Instagram:** Best for visually-driven businesses like fashion, beauty, fitness, food, and lifestyle. If your business relies on high-quality images or videos (such as product photos, tutorials, or behind-the-scenes content), Instagram is a great platform to showcase your brand.

- **Facebook:** Facebook has a broad user base, making it suitable for almost any business. It's particularly useful for businesses that have a local presence or are focused on building community engagement through groups, events, or customer interaction.

- **LinkedIn:** LinkedIn is ideal for businesses in the professional services, B2B (business-to-business), or education sectors. It's great for thought leadership, connecting with industry peers, and targeting professionals who might benefit from your services.

- **TikTok:** TikTok is a rapidly growing platform with a younger audience. It's best for businesses that want to create fun, short-form videos or viral content. Brands in industries like entertainment, fashion, beauty, and food can especially benefit from TikTok's engagement-driven format.

- **Twitter:** Twitter is ideal for real-time engagement, conversations, and sharing industry news. It's great for businesses that want to showcase their expertise, interact with customers, or participate in trending topics.

- **Pinterest:** Pinterest is highly visual and works well for businesses in the fashion, home décor, DIY, and food industries. If your business involves products or ideas that people want to **pin** for future reference, Pinterest can drive a lot of traffic to your site.

Tip: Don't spread yourself too thin by trying to be everywhere. Focus on **one or two platforms** that align with your audience and goals. You can always expand to others later as your business grows.

2. Set Up Professional Profiles

Your social media profiles are often the first impression potential customers have of your business. Make sure your profiles are **professional, on-brand,** and reflect the **personality** and **mission** of your business.

Here's how to set up your profiles effectively:

- **Profile Picture & Cover Image:** Use your **logo** as your profile picture for consistent branding across platforms. Your cover image (if applicable) should reflect your business's tone and can feature your products, a brand slogan, or promotional content.

- **Business Information:** Ensure your bio or "About" section clearly states what your business does, who it serves, and what makes you unique. Keep it short, clear, and to the point. Include a link to your website or a landing page for easy access to more information.

- **Contact Information:** Make it easy for followers to get in touch by providing contact information or linking to your contact page. If your platform allows, add a **"Contact"** button or enable direct messaging to streamline communication.

- **Brand Consistency:** Use the same colors, fonts, and messaging style across all platforms. This creates a cohesive brand identity that's instantly recognizable. Even though each platform has its own vibe, your visuals and tone should feel consistent across your profiles.

3. Plan Your Initial Content Strategy

Having a clear content strategy from the start will help you stay organized and consistent in your social media efforts. While you don't need a fully detailed plan just yet, a basic strategy will guide you in producing relevant content that resonates with your audience and aligns with your business goals.

Here's how to start:

- **Define Your Goals:** What do you want to achieve with social media? Is it **brand awareness, community engagement, lead generation,** or **sales**? Defining your goals helps you tailor your content to meet these objectives. For example, if your goal is to generate leads, you might share helpful resources or guides to drive traffic to your website.

- **Content Types:** Plan to mix up the types of content you share to keep things fresh and engaging. Some ideas include:

  - **Behind-the-scenes content** (showing your work process, office space, or team culture)

- **Product features or demos** (highlighting new or popular products)

- **Customer testimonials** (building trust and social proof)

- **Educational content** (how-to guides, tips, or industry insights)

- **User-generated content** (sharing customer photos or reviews)

- **Interactive content** (polls, questions, and challenges)

- **Posting Frequency:** Be consistent, but don't overcommit. Start with a **manageable posting schedule** that you can stick to. It could be 2-3 times per week to start, depending on the platform and your availability. It's better to post consistently a few times a week than to post sporadically and risk losing momentum.

- **Engagement:** Social media is about conversation, not just broadcasting your message. Respond to comments, like and share relevant content from others, and engage with your audience. Building relationships on social media is key to fostering customer loyalty.

- **Hashtags:** Hashtags help increase the visibility of your posts. Research relevant hashtags for your industry, and include a mix of popular and niche hashtags in your posts. For example, if you're in the fitness industry, you could use #fitness, #healthylifestyle, or #fitfam.

Establishing a strong social media presence doesn't need to be complicated or time-consuming. By **selecting platforms** that are most relevant to your audience, **setting up professional profiles**, and **planning an initial content strategy**, you can begin building your online community and connecting with customers in no time. Remember, consistency and authenticity are key—don't aim for perfection; aim for progress and engagement with your followers.

Reaching Your Target Audience

Develop a Clear Marketing Message

A clear, compelling marketing message is the foundation of how you communicate your value to potential customers. It's what makes your business stand out from the competition and grabs your audience's attention. But in order to truly connect with your audience, your message must speak directly to their needs, desires, and pain points. In this section, we'll cover how to **focus on benefits over features, use language that resonates with your audience**, and **highlight your unique value** to craft a marketing message that drives action.

1. Focus on Benefits, Not Features

One of the most common mistakes businesses make is talking too much about their **features**—the technical aspects or characteristics of their products or services. While features are important, **benefits** are what truly sell. Benefits answer the question, "How does this product or service improve my life?"

Here's the difference:

- **Feature:** "Our fitness app tracks your daily steps."

- **Benefit:** "Our fitness app helps you stay on track with your health goals, making it easier to stay fit and feel your best."

People don't buy products or services because of the features—they buy because of the **end result** the product delivers. So, when crafting your marketing message, always frame your offering in terms of how it benefits your audience. Think about what **problem** your product or service solves or what **desire** it fulfills. This will help you connect on a deeper level with potential customers.

2. Use Language That Resonates with Your Audience

The language you use in your marketing message needs to align with your audience's **tone, values,** and **interests.** It's important to **speak their language,** not just the language of your industry. Your customers want to feel like you understand them and their challenges—so the more your message reflects their mindset, the more likely they are to engage with your brand.

Here's how to ensure your message resonates:

- **Understand Your Audience's Pain Points:** What keeps them up at night? What challenges are they facing? Whether you're solving a specific problem or offering a desired outcome, your language should address these needs head-on.

- **Use Simple, Clear Language**: Avoid jargon or overly technical language that may confuse or alienate your audience. Keep your messaging **simple** and **direct**—speak to the core desire or problem your customer has in a way that's easy to understand.

- **Speak to Their Emotions**: People often make purchasing decisions based on emotions, not logic. Your marketing message should tap into the **emotions** your audience feels around their problem or need. For example, if you're offering a service that helps people improve their financial health, you might speak to the emotions of **security, peace of mind**, or **freedom** that your service can provide.

3. Highlight Your Unique Value

To stand out from the competition, your marketing message must clearly communicate what makes you different—your **unique value proposition** (UVP). Your UVP is what sets your business apart and gives people a reason to choose you over others.

Here's how to craft a strong UVP:

- **Identify What Makes You Different**: What do you offer that others don't? Whether it's a unique feature, a special offer, or an aspect of your customer experience, make sure your UVP is clear in your marketing message. For example, if you offer faster shipping, personalized customer service, or an exclusive product, make that a central part of your message.

- **Make It Specific and Relevant**: Generic statements like "we offer great customer service" don't differentiate you enough. Instead, be specific about how your offering stands out. For example, "We guarantee next-day delivery on all orders" is much more compelling and sets clear expectations.

- **Tie Your UVP to the Customer's Needs**: Your UVP should be directly tied to the **benefits** your customers care about. Don't just tell them what makes you different— show them how it makes their life better.

For example, if your business offers eco-friendly products, your UVP could highlight your commitment to sustainability and appeal to customers who value environmentally conscious choices.

A strong marketing message is the key to attracting the right customers and standing out in a crowded market. By **focusing on benefits instead of features**, **using language that resonates with your audience**, and **highlighting your unique value,** you can craft a message that speaks directly to your customers' needs and motivates them to take action.

Remember, your marketing message should always evolve based on feedback from your customers. If your audience responds well to a certain angle or phrase, keep refining your message to reflect that.

Use Low-Cost Marketing Strategies

Marketing your new business doesn't have to break the bank. In fact, many **low-cost marketing strategies** can be incredibly effective, especially when you're just starting out and need to maximize your budget. By leveraging **social** media, **email marketing**, **influencers**, and **special offers**, you can generate awareness, build trust, and attract customers—all while keeping your costs low. Let's dive into some of the most cost-effective marketing strategies to help you grow your business on a budget.

1. Leverage Social Media and Email Marketing

Both **social media** and **email marketing** are powerful tools for reaching your audience, and the best part is, they don't have to cost anything beyond your time and effort. Here's how to use them effectively:

- **Social Media Marketing:**
  Social media is a goldmine for free promotion, allowing you to engage directly with your target audience. Here's how to make the most of it:

  - **Consistency is Key:** Post regularly on the platforms you've chosen, whether it's Instagram, Facebook, LinkedIn, or Twitter. Share a mix of content—educational posts, behind-the-scenes looks, customer testimonials, and promotional offers.

- ○ **Engage with Your Followers:** Respond to comments, share user-generated content, and participate in conversations. Engaging with your followers builds relationships and trust, which can lead to sales and brand loyalty.

- ○ **Use Hashtags Wisely:** Hashtags help your content reach a wider audience. Research and use relevant hashtags in your niche to increase visibility. Don't overuse them; focus on quality over quantity.

- ○ **Run Contests or Giveaways:** Contests are a great way to quickly grow your social media following and increase engagement. Offering a prize related to your business (e.g., a free product or service) can attract potential customers and generate buzz.

- **Email Marketing:**
Email marketing remains one of the most effective ways to nurture relationships

with your audience and convert leads into customers. Here's how to get started:

- **Build Your Email List:** Start collecting emails as soon as possible, whether through your website, social media, or a lead magnet (like a free eBook or discount). Make sure you're complying with GDPR or any other relevant data protection regulations.

- **Segment Your List:** Not all subscribers are the same. Segment your email list based on customer behavior, location, or interests so you can send targeted, personalized messages.

- **Craft Compelling Emails:** Focus on creating value with every email. Share valuable content, product updates, or exclusive offers. Keep your messages clear and concise, with a strong call-to-action.

- **Automate Email Campaigns:** Tools like Mailchimp or ConvertKit allow

you to automate welcome
sequences, promotional emails, and
reminders, saving you time while
maintaining consistent
communication with your
audience.

2. Collaborate with Influencers or Affiliates

Influencer and affiliate marketing don't need to
cost a fortune. By collaborating with **micro-
influencers** or **affiliates**, you can tap into their
established audiences without breaking your
budget. Here's how to get started:

- **Find Micro-Influencers in Your Niche:**
  Micro-influencers (those with 1,000 to
  100,000 followers) typically have highly
  engaged audiences and are more
  affordable than larger influencers. Look
  for influencers who align with your brand
  values and target audience. Even if you
  offer them a **free product** or a **small fee**,
  they can help you get in front of potential
  customers.

- **Offer Affiliate Partnerships:** If you have
  products or services that people can
  promote, consider starting an **affiliate**

program where influencers or partners earn a commission on sales they generate. Affiliate marketing is performance-based, meaning you only pay for actual sales, which minimizes financial risk.

- **Provide Value in Exchange for Exposure:** Influencers and affiliates don't always need monetary compensation. If you have a product that they'll find useful or a service that aligns with their audience, offer it for free in exchange for a review or a mention. Many influencers are willing to promote products they genuinely like, especially in niche markets.

3. Offer Introductory Discounts or Trials

Offering special discounts or trials is a great way to entice new customers to try your product or service, while also creating urgency around your offer. Here's how to make the most of it:

- **Introductory Discounts:** Offer a **discount for first-time customers,** such as 10% off or a buy-one-get-one-free deal. This can be an effective way to attract initial interest, and customers who are happy with their first experience may return for repeat purchases. You can promote these discounts through your website, social media, and email marketing.

- **Free Trials or Samples:** If your business offers a service, consider offering a **free trial** or **demo**. If you sell products, offering free samples can be a great way to entice people to try before they buy. A no-risk offer makes potential customers more likely to take the plunge.

- **Limited-Time Offers:** Create urgency by offering **time-limited promotions**. A discount or bonus offer that expires in a week can prompt people to act quickly. You could also run flash sales or seasonal promotions to keep things exciting and encourage immediate purchases.

Using **low-cost marketing strategies** is a smart way to build awareness, attract customers, and grow your business without a large advertising budget. By **leveraging social media and email marketing**, **collaborating with influencers or affiliates**, and **offering introductory discounts or trials**, you can drive traffic to your business and build a loyal customer base.

Remember, the key to successful low-cost marketing is **creativity** and **consistency**. Focus on delivering value to your customers, and over time, your efforts will pay off.

Build Relationships with Early Customers

Your first customers are not just people who buy from you—they are **partners** in your journey and a critical part of your startup's success. Building strong, lasting relationships with your early customers can lead to **repeat business, referrals**, and a solid foundation of **brand advocates**. By taking the time to engage with them, show appreciation, and gather feedback, you'll create a loyal customer base that will help your business thrive. This section covers the key actions you can take to **respond promptly, showcase testimonials**, and **reward loyalty** in ways that build trust and long-term relationships.

1. Respond Promptly to Inquiries

Customer experience plays a significant role in how your business is perceived. One of the easiest ways to build a relationship with your early customers is by responding to their questions or concerns in a timely, professional manner.

- **Set Clear Expectations:** Let your customers know how soon they can expect a response. Whether you promise to respond within 24 hours or 48 hours, be clear about your timelines so customers aren't left waiting in the dark.

- **Be Friendly and Approachable:** When communicating with early customers, it's important to be warm, polite, and helpful. Even if their inquiry seems minor, treat it as a priority. Make your customers feel valued from the very first interaction.

- **Offer Personalized Responses:** Instead of sending generic replies, personalize your messages. For instance, use their name and refer specifically to their query. This shows you're paying attention to their needs and are committed to providing value.

- **Set Up Automated Responses (Where Appropriate):** If you have a high volume of inquiries, setting up automated emails or a chatbot can ensure that customers receive an immediate acknowledgment of their inquiry. Just make sure you follow up personally once you can provide a more detailed response.

2. Request and Showcase Testimonials

Early customers are a goldmine for social proof—when you deliver a great product or service, they can help build credibility for your brand. Testimonials from satisfied customers provide authenticity and encourage new prospects to trust your business.

- **Ask for Feedback:** After a customer has received your product or service, follow up and ask for their feedback. This can be in the form of a short survey or a request for a testimonial. Keep it simple and straightforward, asking for their honest opinion about what they liked, what could be improved, and how your offering helped them.

- **Make It Easy for Customers to Share:** Provide a simple way for customers to leave testimonials. This could be through an online review platform (Google Reviews, Trustpilot, etc.), via a direct email, or a testimonial form on your website. If possible, ask for testimonials in multiple formats—written, video, or even photos of them using your product.

- **Showcase Testimonials Across Your Channels:** Once you've received positive testimonials, use them to build your credibility. Display them prominently on your website, include them in marketing materials, and share them on social media. Video testimonials or photos of satisfied customers with your product can be especially powerful. Customer testimonials not only build trust but also act as a form of free advertising for your business.

3. Reward Loyalty with Special Offers

One of the most effective ways to build strong, long-lasting relationships with customers is by showing appreciation for their support. Rewarding loyalty not only keeps customers happy but also encourages them to return, refer others, and continue advocating for your brand.

- **Offer Exclusive Discounts for Repeat Customers:** Consider creating a loyalty program that rewards customers for their repeat business. You could offer discounts on future purchases, access to special promotions, or even a "VIP" membership with extra perks. For example, "Get 15% off your next purchase when you shop again within 30 days."

- **Surprise and Delight with Unexpected Gifts:** Occasionally sending a small gift or handwritten note to a loyal customer can have a lasting impact. This gesture shows that you value their business beyond just a transaction. It could be a free sample, a discount code for a friend, or a special thank-you gift for their support.

- **Referral Bonuses:** Encourage your loyal customers to share your business with their friends and family by offering **referral bonuses**. For example, offer both the referrer and the new customer a discount or free product when a purchase is made through a referral link. This helps to turn your best customers into advocates for your brand and can create a network of customers who are both loyal and actively recommending your business.

- **Create a Sense of Community:** Rewarding loyalty can also mean making your customers feel like they're part of something bigger. Create a sense of belonging through community-building activities, such as exclusive webinars, private Facebook groups, or members-only events. This deepens the emotional connection between your customers and your brand.

Building strong relationships with your early customers is crucial to your long-term success. By **responding promptly** to their inquiries, **showcasing testimonials** to build credibility, and **rewarding loyalty** with special offers, you can foster a loyal, engaged customer base that will support your business as it grows. These relationships aren't just transactions—they are partnerships that will help sustain your startup for years to come.

Take the time to nurture these early relationships, and you'll see the rewards in the form of customer retention, word-of-mouth referrals, and a strong brand reputation.

"...respond promptly, showcase testimonials, and reward loyalty..."

Creating a Simple Sales Funnel

Attract Potential Customers

Attracting potential customers is about **getting in front of the right audience** and capturing their interest. It's not just about selling—it's about providing value, creating trust, and forming connections. With the right strategies, you can bring in customers who are genuinely interested in what you offer, even on a small budget. In this section, we'll explore how to **use engaging posts or ads**, **share free resources**, and **participate in relevant online communities** to effectively attract your ideal customers.

1. Use Engaging Posts or Ads

Whether through organic social media posts or paid ads, creating **engaging content** is one of the most effective ways to attract potential customers. The goal is to spark interest and make your audience want to learn more about your business.

- **Craft Compelling Content:** When creating posts or ads, focus on creating content that **engages** your audience, rather than just promoting your product. Share **useful tips, industry insights,** or **behind-the-scenes looks** that showcase your expertise. Make your content informative, entertaining, or inspiring so that it resonates with your target audience.

- **Use Visuals:** Posts with eye-catching images, videos, or infographics tend to attract more attention. You don't need a professional photographer to create stunning visuals—tools like Canva or Adobe Spark allow you to design high-quality graphics easily and quickly. **Video content,** whether it's a product demo, tutorial, or customer testimonial, can be especially engaging.

- **Create Interactive Content:** Engage your audience with polls, quizzes, and questions. People love participating in content that invites them to share their opinions. This not only helps you understand your audience better, but also increases engagement and builds community around your brand.

- **Paid Ads**: If you have a small budget for paid marketing, start with **targeted ads** on social media platforms (such as Facebook or Instagram) or Google. These platforms offer detailed targeting options that allow you to reach people based on demographics, behaviors, or even specific interests. Start with a small budget, test different ad creatives, and monitor your results to see which ads perform the best.

2. Share Free Resources to Build Trust

Giving away something valuable for free can be a powerful tool to build **trust** and **establish authority** in your industry. Free resources not only attract potential customers but also show that you're genuinely interested in providing value before asking for anything in return.

- **Create Lead Magnets**: Lead magnets are valuable pieces of content (eBooks, checklists, templates, etc.) that you offer in exchange for a potential customer's contact information, usually their email address. Make sure your lead magnet is highly relevant to your audience's needs. For example, if you're offering a fitness product, a free workout guide or meal planner would be a great lead magnet.

- **Offer Free Webinars or Workshops**: Hosting a live or recorded webinar is a great way to build trust while sharing your expertise. Offer a **free training session** on a topic that's relevant to your target audience. The key is to provide actionable value—people are much more likely to trust your business if you show them how knowledgeable and helpful you are.

- **Publish Blog Posts and Articles**: If you have a blog, use it to create content that addresses the questions and challenges your potential customers face. Provide helpful advice, industry trends, and solutions to common problems. By positioning yourself as a trusted source of information, you'll increase your chances of attracting potential customers who see value in what you offer.

- **Offer Free Trials or Samples**: If your business model allows it, offering **free**

trials of your product or service can be an incredibly effective way to gain traction. A free trial lowers the risk for customers and gives them the chance to experience your product first-hand, which often leads to paid conversions once they see the value.

3. Participate in Relevant Online Communities

Your potential customers are already participating in online communities—they may be on Facebook groups, Reddit threads, industry-specific forums, or LinkedIn discussions. By actively engaging in these communities, you can connect with your target audience in a natural, authentic way.

- **Join Niche Communities**: Focus on finding and joining online groups, forums, or social media communities that are directly related to your industry or the interests of your target audience. For example, if you sell eco-friendly products, join sustainability-focused groups or forums where people are talking about environmental issues.

- **Provide Value in Discussions**: Don't just promote your business—**engage genuinely**.

Offer advice, answer questions, and provide solutions without expecting immediate sales. Share your expertise in a helpful, non-salesy way. This positions you as a knowledgeable resource and builds trust within the community.

- **Be Consistent but Subtle:** Consistency is key when participating in online communities. The more you contribute, the more you build your reputation. However, be subtle about promoting your business. Share your business only when it's relevant to the conversation or when someone specifically asks for a recommendation. Over-promotion can quickly turn people off.

- **Host Q&A Sessions or AMAs (Ask Me Anything):** On platforms like Reddit or LinkedIn, you can host Q&A sessions where you answer specific questions related to your industry or area of expertise. This is an excellent way to build authority and get your brand in front of potential customers.

Attracting potential customers doesn't require large-scale ad campaigns or an extensive marketing budget. By **using engaging posts or ads**, **sharing free resources**, and **participating in relevant online communities**, you can effectively draw in a steady stream of new customers. These strategies will help you build trust, establish authority, and create long-term relationships with the people who need your products or services.

The key is consistency. As you continue to create value and engage with your audience, your reputation will grow, leading to more opportunities to convert potential customers into loyal ones.

You have made excellent progress in this book. I admire your dedication and perseverance and this will serve you very well in your business journey. As a reminder, I am a self-published author and count on reviews from people like you. If you have a few minutes, please log onto Amazon and leave me a review. I would really appreciate it!

As a thank you for your support, I would like to offer you a surprise business gift to assist you. Please scan the code below from a mobile device to connect with me and claim your gift.

The QR code above will lead you to the following website:
https://mailchi.mp/e49730aa7f68/start-a-business-in-10-minutes-a-day

---

Convert Leads into Paying Customers

Once you've attracted potential customers, the next crucial step is to **convert those leads into paying customers.** Conversions are the lifeblood of your business, and they require a thoughtful, strategic approach. In this section, we'll cover three key tactics to help you **close the deal** and turn interested prospects into loyal buyers: **offering easy checkout options, creating urgency with limited-time offers,** and **providing exceptional customer support.**

1. Offer Easy Checkout Options

The checkout process is the final hurdle between your potential customer and a sale. If the process is complicated, long, or unclear, you risk losing the sale. To increase conversions, **simplify** the checkout experience as much as possible.

- **Streamline the Process**: Keep the checkout process short and user-friendly. Only ask for the essential information. Ideally, the customer should be able to complete the purchase in **three to five steps.** If you ask for too many details, they may abandon the cart.

- **Offer Multiple Payment Methods**: Make sure you offer a variety of payment options that are convenient for your target audience. Some customers prefer credit/debit cards, while others might want to use **PayPal, Apple Pay,** or even **buy now, pay later** options like **Klarna** or **Afterpay.** Providing flexibility can reduce friction and increase conversions.

- **Include Guest Checkout**: Don't force customers to create an account to complete a purchase unless it's absolutely necessary. While account creation can be valuable for customer retention, many first-time buyers prefer the option to **check out as guests** for convenience.

- **Provide Clear Pricing and Shipping Information**: Surprises at checkout can cause customers to abandon their purchase. Be transparent about pricing, shipping costs, and estimated delivery times before the final checkout step. If customers know exactly what they're paying for and when they can expect delivery, they're more likely to follow through.

- **Use Cart Abandonment Reminders**: If someone adds items to their cart but doesn't complete the purchase, send them a **cart abandonment email** or push notification. Offer a gentle reminder of their abandoned items, and perhaps include an incentive like a discount or free shipping to encourage them to return and complete the sale.

2. Create Urgency with Limited-Time Offers

Urgency is a psychological trigger that can help move potential customers from hesitation to action. By creating a sense of urgency around your offer, you can encourage leads to **act quickly** rather than procrastinate.

- **Flash Sales**: A **flash sale** is a limited-time offer, typically lasting from a few hours to a couple of days. Flash sales create excitement and motivate customers to make a purchase now rather than wait. To maximize impact, promote your flash sale through email, social media, and your website.

- **Countdown Timers**: On your website or in email promotions, include a **countdown timer** that shows how much time is left in a sale or offer. This visual representation of time running out is a powerful motivator and can push hesitant buyers to act quickly.

- **Limited Quantity Offers**: Scarcity is another powerful motivator. Use phrases like "Only 10 items left!" or "Limited stock available" to make customers feel like they're missing out if they don't act fast. This can create a sense of urgency to purchase before the item sells out.

- **Special Launch or Seasonal Offers**: If you're launching a new product or service, or if it's a busy time of year like the holidays, offer a **limited-time discount** to create urgency around your new release.

This encourages customers to try your product before the price goes back up.

3. Provide Exceptional Customer Support

Great customer service is the key to turning one-time buyers into **repeat customers** and **brand advocates.** When customers feel valued, supported, and heard, they are far more likely to complete a purchase and return in the future.

- **Be Available and Responsive**: Provide multiple channels for customers to reach you, such as **email, live chat**, and **social media.** Make sure you respond quickly to inquiries and resolve issues promptly. Fast responses show customers that you value their time and business.

- **Personalize Interactions**: Treat your customers as individuals. Address them by their names and tailor your communication to their specific needs or concerns. This personal touch can go a long way in creating a positive, lasting relationship.

- **Resolve Issues Quickly**: If a customer has an issue—whether it's with a product, service, or order—resolve it as quickly as possible. Offering **hassle-free returns, quick refunds,** or even **exchanges** helps to build trust and shows that you stand behind your product.

- **Offer Post-Purchase Support**: Customer service shouldn't end once the sale is completed. Provide post-purchase support to help customers use your product effectively. This could include **how-to guides, FAQ pages,** or offering direct support through email or phone. Additionally, send a **thank-you email** to show appreciation and remind them of your contact info if they need help.

- **Request Feedback and Act on It**: After a customer makes a purchase, ask for their feedback. Use surveys or simple follow-up emails to learn about their experience. Not only does this show that you care about their opinion, but it also provides you with valuable insights into areas where you can improve. Act on this feedback to continually refine your offerings and customer experience.

Converting leads into paying customers is the final step in your marketing journey, and it's essential for the long-term success of your business. By **offering easy checkout options, creating urgency with limited-time offers,** and **providing exceptional customer support,** you can reduce friction in the buying process, encourage faster decisions, and build a loyal customer base that will continue to support your business.

Remember, each interaction you have with a potential customer is an opportunity to build trust, demonstrate value, and turn that lead into a **repeat buyer.** Keep the customer experience smooth, convenient, and positive, and your conversion rates will improve over time.

Retain and Upsell to Existing Customers

Your existing customers are not just a source of revenue—they're your **most valuable asset.** They've already experienced the value you offer, and they're more likely to buy from you again than new customers are. By **retaining** your current customer base and **upselling** complementary products or services, you can significantly increase your revenue while building stronger relationships. In this section, we'll cover three key strategies to help you retain and upsell to existing customers: **collecting feedback to improve**, **suggesting complementary products or services**, and **offering loyalty incentives**.

1. Collect Feedback to Improve

Feedback from your current customers is invaluable—it gives you insights into what's working, what's not, and where you can improve. By actively listening to your customers, you can refine your offerings, fix issues, and provide an even better experience.

- **Surveys and Reviews:** Send out short surveys or follow-up emails after a purchase to collect feedback on your product or service. Ask for specific input about what your customers liked, what they didn't like, and how you can improve. Simple questions like "How would you rate your experience?" or "What could we do better?" can provide actionable insights.

- **Listen to Complaints:** While it's easy to focus on positive feedback, **customer complaints** are equally valuable. Addressing issues head-on, whether it's product quality, delivery times, or customer service, not only resolves problems but can turn a dissatisfied customer into a loyal advocate. **Quickly resolve complaints** and let your customers know you're committed to providing a better experience.

- **Monitor Social Media and Forums**: Keep an eye on what customers are saying about you online. Social media platforms, online reviews, and industry forums can provide a wealth of feedback. Respond to comments and messages to show that you care about their opinions and that you're actively improving based on their suggestions.

- **Use Feedback to Innovate**: Don't just collect feedback—**act on it**. Use the insights you gain to improve your products, services, or customer experience. Customers appreciate seeing their feedback make a difference, and this makes them feel valued and more likely to stay loyal to your brand.

2. Suggest Complementary Products or Services

Once you've built trust with your customers, you can encourage them to purchase again by suggesting **complementary products** or **services** that align with their previous purchase. This is an excellent way to **upsell** and increase the value of each customer.

- **Product Bundles**: Offer bundled products or services that make sense together. For example, if a customer buys a fitness tracker, you could upsell accessories like a carrying case, extra bands, or even an online fitness program. Bundle deals often appear more attractive and offer customers better value for their money.

- **Personalized Recommendations**: Use your customer data to suggest products based on past purchases or browsing behavior. If you're running an online store, recommend related items on the checkout page or in follow-up emails. Personalized suggestions help customers find products they might not have otherwise discovered, increasing the likelihood of additional sales.

- **Time-Based Upselling**: If your business offers subscriptions or services, offer a time-based upsell. For example, after a customer has had time to use your product or service, reach out with an offer for an **upgraded plan, premium features,** or a complementary add-on. Timing is key— approach customers when they're most likely to appreciate the added value.

- **Cross-Sell at the Point of Purchase**: When a customer is completing a transaction, provide them with complementary products or services to enhance their purchase. For instance, "Add this extended warranty for just $10 more" or "Get 20% off these accessories when you purchase today." These suggestions make it easier for customers to buy additional items that complement their needs.

3. Offer Loyalty Incentives

Rewarding your existing customers is one of the most effective ways to retain them and keep them coming back for more. Loyalty incentives not only show appreciation but also encourage repeat purchases and long-term relationships.

- **Loyalty Programs**: Create a **rewards program** where customers earn points or discounts for every purchase they make. Customers love feeling like they're getting something extra for their loyalty. For example, offer **1 point for every dollar spent,** and allow customers to redeem those points for discounts or exclusive products once they reach a certain threshold.

- **Exclusive Discounts**: Offer **special discounts or perks** to repeat customers. For instance, send out an email offering 10% off their next purchase as a thank-you for their business. You can also create VIP-only promotions or early access to sales to make your loyal customers feel appreciated and special.

- **Referral Programs**: Encourage your existing customers to refer new customers by offering incentives for successful referrals. A **referral program** could include a discount or free product for both the referrer and the new customer. This not only helps with customer retention but also encourages word-of-mouth marketing, which can be highly effective.

- **Surprise Gifts or Offers**: Occasionally surprise your loyal customers with **free samples, birthday gifts,** or unexpected discounts. These "surprise and delight" tactics can have a lasting impact on customer satisfaction and loyalty. Small gestures go a long way in making customers feel valued and appreciated.

Retaining and upselling to existing customers is an excellent way to boost revenue and build long-term relationships. By **collecting feedback to improve, suggesting complementary products or services,** and **offering loyalty incentives,** you can encourage repeat business, increase customer lifetime value, and create a thriving, loyal customer base that supports your business growth.

The key is to keep providing value—whether that's through improved products, personalized recommendations, or exclusive rewards. When you treat customers like partners and continue to meet their needs, they'll keep coming back, and they'll often bring others along with them.

CHAPTER 4

Managing and Growing Your Business

Tracking Your Progress

Personally, I love getting to the place in a new business where you can track data. You can start to tell a story, make improvements and identify gaps. This is also the part where you can start to see glimpses of potential and, in some cases, really enjoy it!

Set Up Simple Tracking Tools

To run your business efficiently, it's crucial to keep track of key metrics that will inform your decisions and help you measure progress. Setting up **simple tracking tools** can give you valuable insights without overwhelming you with complex systems. In this section, we'll cover three essential tracking tools: **using a spreadsheet for sales and expenses, monitoring website and social media analytics,** and **tracking customer engagement metrics.**

1. Use a Spreadsheet for Sales and Expenses

One of the easiest and most effective ways to start tracking your business's financials is by setting up a **simple spreadsheet.** Spreadsheets allow you to manage your **sales** and **expenses** without needing complicated accounting software.

- **Track Sales and Revenue:** Create columns for **sales date, customer name, product/service sold,** and **amount received.** You can also categorize your sales based on different product lines or customer segments to gain insights into what's driving your revenue. For example, if you sell multiple products, track which ones are performing best.

- **Monitor Expenses**: Similarly, track your **business expenses** such as **supplies**, **marketing costs**, **software subscriptions**, and **operating costs**. Set up columns for **expense type**, **amount spent**, and **date**. This will help you stay on top of your budget and ensure you're not overspending.

- **Profit and Loss Calculation**: Use your sales and expenses data to calculate your monthly **profit and loss (P&L)**. Simply subtract your total expenses from your total revenue to determine if your business is profitable. This basic calculation will give you a snapshot of your business's financial health.

- **Track Cash Flow**: Keeping an eye on cash flow is essential for understanding your business's liquidity. In your spreadsheet, track your **incoming payments** and **outgoing expenses** to ensure you have enough cash to cover costs. A positive cash flow is critical for sustaining operations and funding growth.

- **Use Templates**: If you're new to spreadsheets, there are many free templates available online for tracking sales and expenses. Tools like **Google Sheets** or **Microsoft Excel** offer built-in templates, and you can customize them to suit your business needs.

2. Monitor Website and Social Media Analytics

Your website and social media channels are key touchpoints for customer engagement and sales. By regularly monitoring **website** and **social media analytics**, you can see what's working and what needs improvement, helping you optimize your marketing efforts.

- **Website Analytics**: Use tools like **Google Analytics** to track your website traffic and performance. Key metrics to watch include:

  - **Page views**: See how many people are visiting your site and which pages are most popular.

- ○ **Bounce rate:** Track the percentage of visitors who leave your site after viewing only one page. A high bounce rate may indicate that your landing page needs improvement.

- ○ **Conversion rate:** Measure how many visitors take action, such as signing up for your email list or making a purchase. A high conversion rate indicates that your website is effective at guiding visitors toward a specific action.

- ○ **Referral sources:** Understand where your traffic is coming from—whether it's from social media, search engines, or paid ads. This can help you focus your marketing efforts on the most successful channels.

- **Social Media Analytics:** Each social platform provides analytics that show how your content is performing. For example:

- ○ **Facebook Insights:** Track engagement with your posts, including likes, comments, shares, and the reach of your posts.

- ○ **Instagram Analytics**: See how well your posts are performing in terms of impressions, reach, and engagement (likes, comments, saves).

- ○ **Twitter Analytics**: Track your tweet impressions, engagement rate, and follower growth.

- **Key Metrics to Track**: Focus on metrics like **engagement** (likes, shares, comments), **growth rate** (new followers), and **click-through rate (CTR)** for links you share. These metrics give you an idea of how well your content is resonating with your audience and whether your social media efforts are translating into traffic or sales.

- **Schedule Regular Check-Ins**: Set aside a few minutes each week to check your website and social media analytics. Regular monitoring allows you to identify trends, track improvements, and adjust your strategies when necessary.

3. Track Customer Engagement Metrics

Tracking how your customers interact with your business will give you valuable insights into their behaviors and preferences. This can help you improve your marketing and sales strategies to better meet their needs.

- **Email Open and Click Rates**: If you're using email marketing to reach customers, track **open rates** (how many people opened your emails) and **click rates** (how many clicked on links within your emails). These metrics will help you assess whether your subject lines and content are compelling enough to drive engagement.

- **Customer Satisfaction (CSAT)**: After each transaction or customer service interaction, ask customers for feedback on their experience. This can be a quick survey or a simple rating system (e.g., 1 to 5 stars). Tracking **customer satisfaction scores** can help you identify areas for improvement and gauge how happy your customers are with your business.

- **Net Promoter Score (NPS)**: The NPS is a simple yet effective tool to measure customer loyalty. Ask customers how likely they are to recommend your business to others on a scale from 0 to 10. Those who score 9-10 are **promoters,** those who score 7-8 are **passives,** and those who score 0-6 are **detractors**. Tracking your NPS over time can help you understand how loyal your customers are.

- **Customer Retention Rate:** Measure how many customers make repeat purchases over time. A high **customer retention rate** is a good indicator of business success and customer satisfaction. You can calculate it by dividing the number of customers you have at the end of a period (minus new customers) by the number you had at the beginning.

- **Engagement with Your Offers:** Track how customers are engaging with your offers, promotions, and discounts. For example, if you sent out a special offer email, track how many customers used the coupon code and made a purchase. This helps you understand the effectiveness of your promotional efforts.

Setting up simple tracking tools is essential for maintaining control over your business's performance. By using a **spreadsheet for sales and expenses, monitoring website and social media analytics,** and **tracking customer engagement metrics,** you'll be able to make data-driven decisions that drive growth and profitability.

Tracking doesn't have to be complex or time-consuming. With just a few basic tools, you can gain valuable insights into what's working, identify areas for improvement, and stay on top of your goals. The more you track, the easier it becomes to adjust and refine your strategies for long-term success.

Review Your Progress Weekly

Regularly reviewing your progress is key to ensuring that your business stays on track and that you're continually improving. **Weekly reviews** help you stay aligned with your goals, assess what's working, and identify areas for improvement. In this section, we'll cover how to **compare actual outcomes to goals, identify areas for improvement,** and **adjust your plan as needed.**

1. Compare Actual Outcomes to Goals

At the end of each week, take time to compare your **actual outcomes** with the goals you set in your business plan. This will help you gauge whether you're making progress and if you need to adjust your approach.

- **Track Key Metrics**: Look at the **key metrics** you've been tracking, such as **sales, website traffic, social media engagement**, and **customer feedback**. Compare these figures to the goals you set for the week. Are you meeting your sales targets? Is your website traffic increasing as expected? Are customers engaging with your content?

- **Set SMART Goals**: Make sure your goals are **SMART**—Specific, Measurable, Achievable, Relevant, and Time-bound. This makes it easier to compare actual outcomes to your set goals. For example, "Increase sales by 15% this month" is a clear, measurable goal. If you achieve 10%, you know you're getting close, but there's room to grow.

- **Celebrate Wins, Big and Small**: Even if you didn't hit every target, recognize the wins you did achieve. Celebrating small successes helps maintain momentum and motivation. Perhaps you gained more followers than expected or received positive feedback from a customer. These are all signs of progress.

- **Identify Shortcomings**: If you fall short of a goal, don't be discouraged. Look at **what went wrong**—did you miscalculate, underestimate the challenge, or simply not allocate enough time to the task? Reviewing this objectively helps you learn from setbacks.

2. Identify Areas for Improvement

The weekly review is an opportunity to pinpoint areas where you can improve. Running a business is an iterative process, and consistent improvements will help you grow over time.

- **Analyze Your Efforts**: Take a close look at the activities you've been working on. What strategies and actions have been effective? Which ones haven't generated the results you were hoping for? For example, if you've been running social media ads, do they need tweaking, or are they reaching the wrong audience?

- **Look at Feedback**: Pay attention to feedback from customers, team members (if applicable), and any external sources. If you're consistently hearing about the same issue, whether it's related to your product, service, or customer experience, that's a clear sign of an area to improve.

- **Evaluate Time Management**: Reflect on how efficiently you've been using your time. Were there days where you felt too busy or overwhelmed? Could you have spent more time on critical tasks like product development or customer outreach? Identifying time management gaps will help you refine your strategy going forward.

- **Customer Experience**: If your customers aren't engaging or buying as expected, it might be worth reassessing their experience with your business. Are there any friction points in the buying process? Are your offerings clear and compelling? If there's a consistent issue, address it promptly.

3. Adjust Your Plan as Needed

As your business evolves, so too should your plan. The weekly review gives you the chance to **adjust your approach** and ensure that your business is heading in the right direction. This doesn't mean abandoning your original goals, but rather fine-tuning your strategies to optimize results.

- **Adjust Tactics**: Based on what you've learned, consider **adjusting your tactics**. For example, if a particular marketing strategy is not yielding the results you expected, try a different approach. Test different ad creatives, revise your email campaigns, or tweak your social media content to see what resonates more with your audience.

- **Refine Your Goals**: Over time, you may find that your goals need to be **adjusted** as well. Perhaps you've exceeded your expectations and need to set more ambitious goals, or maybe you've realized that a certain objective wasn't as realistic as it seemed. Either way, be open to revising your goals based on the progress you've made and the challenges you face.

- **Focus on Priorities**: After reviewing your progress, take time to **reprioritize** tasks for the upcoming week. Based on the data, identify which areas require more focus and allocate your limited time and resources accordingly. If sales are lagging, for example, you might want to spend more time refining your product page or engaging with potential customers.

- **Test New Ideas**: If something isn't working, don't be afraid to experiment. The beauty of running a startup is the ability to pivot quickly and try new approaches. Whether it's testing a new product offering or exploring a new marketing channel, use your weekly review as an opportunity to **experiment** with fresh ideas.

"...tracking customer engagement metrics, you'll be able to make data-driven decisions that drive growth and profitability."

A **weekly progress review** keeps you accountable and ensures that you're consistently moving forward. By **comparing actual outcomes to goals**, **identifying areas for improvement**, and **adjusting your plan as needed**, you'll maintain a dynamic and adaptable business strategy. This process helps you stay on track, build momentum, and make continuous improvements—ensuring long-term success.

Keep in mind that small weekly adjustments can have a huge impact over time. Each week is an opportunity to learn, refine, and grow your business. The key is to stay consistent with your reviews and be willing to adapt based on what you're seeing.

Celebrate Milestones and Achievements

Building a business is a journey, and like any long-term endeavor, it's important to **celebrate milestones and achievements** along the way. Recognizing both small and large successes helps you stay motivated, reinforces positive behavior, and gives you a sense of progress. This section will focus on how to **recognize small wins to stay motivated**, **share successes with your network**, and **reflect on lessons learned** to keep moving forward with confidence.

1. Recognize Small Wins to Stay Motivated

As a busy entrepreneur, it's easy to get caught up in the bigger goals and overlook the smaller wins that keep the momentum going. However, celebrating **small wins** can be one of the most effective ways to stay motivated and build positive momentum.

- **Celebrate Each Step**: Whether you've secured your first customer, launched a new product, or simply completed a difficult task, take the time to acknowledge your achievements. Small wins add up to big progress, and recognizing them helps you avoid burnout and discouragement.

- **Set Short-Term Milestones**: Break your larger goals into smaller, more manageable tasks. For example, if your goal is to increase sales by 20% in a quarter, set weekly targets to track your progress. Each time you hit a mini milestone—like closing a sale, gaining a new follower, or receiving positive feedback from a customer—celebrate it.

- **Reward Yourself:** Celebrate your victories, no matter how small, with a little reward. Maybe it's a treat you enjoy, a day off, or a small gift to yourself. Positive reinforcement fuels motivation, helping you stay focused and energized for the next challenge.

- **Create a Success Journal:** Keep a **success journal** where you jot down achievements and milestones, no matter how minor they seem. This will give you a sense of accomplishment and provide an invaluable reminder of how far you've come when times get tough.

2. Share Successes with Your Network

Celebrating your milestones isn't just about boosting your morale—it's also about sharing your wins with those around you. **Sharing successes** with your network not only builds credibility and trust but also strengthens relationships with customers, partners, and supporters.

- **Announce Your Achievements:** Share important milestones on your social media platforms, email newsletters, and your website. Whether it's a new product launch, hitting a revenue goal, or gaining a certain number of followers, announcing your wins shows your audience that your business is thriving. It also positions you as someone who's consistently progressing and achieving.

- **Acknowledge Team or Partner Contributions:** If you have a team or business partners, take the time to publicly thank them for their contributions. A simple acknowledgment can go a long way in strengthening relationships and building a positive work environment. If you're a solo entrepreneur, thank your supporters—whether it's friends, family, or mentors—who helped you reach your goal.

- **Use Testimonials and Reviews:** Leverage customer feedback and testimonials as a way to celebrate your business's progress. If you've received positive feedback or a glowing review, share it with your community. Not only does this celebrate your achievements, but it also boosts your reputation and builds trust with potential customers.

- **Celebrate with Your Community**: If you're part of any entrepreneurial networks or communities, don't be shy about sharing your wins. Entrepreneurs support each other, and celebrating success together fosters a sense of camaraderie and helps motivate others in the group.

3. Reflect on Lessons Learned

While celebrating milestones is important, it's equally essential to take a step back and reflect on the **lessons learned** along the way. This helps you gain clarity, avoid repeating mistakes, and refine your approach for continued success.

- **Analyze What Worked**: Take time to reflect on what led to your success. What strategies, actions, or decisions contributed to achieving your milestone? Whether it's a particular marketing tactic, a product change, or a customer outreach strategy, understanding what worked will help you replicate and refine these actions in the future.

- **Learn from Challenges**: Milestones are often accompanied by challenges. Use these moments to learn from any obstacles or setbacks you encountered along the way. Did you face delays? Were there things you could have done differently? **Learning from your mistakes** is just as important as celebrating your wins.

- **Document Key Insights**: After reflecting, document the **lessons learned** and key insights. These can be helpful for future decisions and can act as a roadmap for overcoming similar obstacles down the line. This reflection process allows you to continually grow, improve, and refine your approach to running a business.

- **Apply Your Knowledge**: Once you've recognized what worked and what didn't, take action on your insights. Adjust your strategies or processes to reflect what you've learned. Applying lessons learned will keep you on the path to long-term growth and success.

Celebrating milestones and achievements is not just about boosting morale—it's an essential part of the entrepreneurial journey that helps you stay focused, motivated, and inspired to keep moving forward. By **recognizing small wins, sharing successes with your network,** and **reflecting on lessons learned,** you create a healthy cycle of progress and growth.

In the early stages of your business, it's especially important to **acknowledge every victory,** no matter how small. These celebrations will help you maintain a positive mindset and reinforce the belief that you're making steady progress toward your larger goals.

Keep celebrating the milestones—**they're the building blocks of long-term success!**

Scaling Your Business

Identify Opportunities for Growth

Once your business is up and running, it's time to shift your focus to **growth.** Identifying opportunities for expansion is essential for scaling your business and ensuring long-term success. In this section, we'll explore how to **explore additional revenue streams, expand your target**

audience, and **invest in more efficient tools or resources** to accelerate growth.

1. Explore Additional Revenue Streams

One of the most effective ways to **grow your business** is by introducing **additional revenue streams**. Diversifying your income sources can reduce financial risk and help stabilize your business during lean periods.

- **Complementary Products or Services**: Think about offering **products or services that complement your core offerings**. For example, if you sell handmade jewelry, consider adding jewelry cleaning kits or custom packaging as additional products. If you're providing consulting services, you could create online courses or e-books that provide further value to your clients.

- **Subscription or Recurring Revenue Models**: If your business lends itself to it, consider setting up a **subscription model** where customers pay a recurring fee. This could be a membership program, a subscription box service, or a retainer for ongoing services. Recurring revenue provides a more predictable cash flow and can make financial planning easier.

- **Affiliate Marketing or Partnerships**: If you're not producing all the products or services yourself, consider **affiliate marketing** or forming **partnerships** with other businesses. By promoting products or services that align with your brand, you can earn commissions on sales without directly managing inventory.

- **Seasonal or Limited-Time Offers**: Introducing **seasonal or limited-time offers** can create urgency and drive sales. For instance, offering exclusive discounts, bundles, or holiday-themed products for a short period can help boost revenue during slow months or capitalize on trends.

- **Licensing or Franchising**: If your business model allows, you might explore **licensing your intellectual property** or **franchising** your business. This enables you to scale rapidly by letting other people or companies use your brand, products, or systems in exchange for a fee.

- **Digital Products**: If you have expertise in your field, consider creating **digital products** like e-books, templates, or software tools. These products can be sold online, providing passive income without the overhead of inventory or shipping.

2. Expand Your Target Audience

As your business grows, it's important to continually **expand your target audience**. Reaching new customers and markets helps increase revenue and ensures that your business isn't dependent on a single group of consumers.

- **Segment Your Market**: Analyze your existing customer base and identify **new customer segments** that you haven't yet tapped into. For example, if your primary customers are young professionals, consider targeting **college students** or **older adults** who may also benefit from your products or services.

- **Geographic Expansion**: If you're targeting a local audience, think about expanding your reach to other **regions or countries**. Depending on your product or service, this could involve offering **international**

shipping or targeting customers through digital marketing in new geographic locations.

- **Refine Your Marketing Strategy**: Test different **marketing channels** and **advertising platforms** to reach new people. If you've mainly relied on social media ads, try **search engine optimization (SEO), email marketing**, or **influencer partnerships**. Focus on where your potential customers spend their time and tailor your marketing to fit.

- **Create New Personas**: Understand the **lifestyle, needs**, and **pain points** of different potential customer personas. For instance, if your target audience is mostly women aged 25-35, think about how you can tailor your messaging or product to attract men, or even older women. Testing and refining your customer personas will help you better connect with a wider audience.

- **Leverage Partnerships for New Audiences**: Collaborate with businesses or influencers who already have an established following in different niches. A **cross-promotion** or **joint venture** can help expose your brand to new audiences, expanding your reach without needing to build everything from scratch.

3. Invest in More Efficient Tools or Resources

To scale your business successfully, it's important to **invest in tools and resources** that make your processes more efficient. As your business grows, you'll need better systems to keep up with demand while maintaining quality.

- **Automation Tools**: Invest in **automation tools** that can streamline repetitive tasks and free up your time. For example, use **email marketing platforms** like Mailchimp or ConvertKit to automate campaigns, **social media schedulers** like Buffer or Hootsuite to plan posts in advance, and **CRM software** like HubSpot or Salesforce to manage customer relationships more efficiently.

- **Outsource or Hire Help**: If your workload has become overwhelming, consider **outsourcing tasks** or hiring additional help. Whether it's a virtual assistant to handle customer support or a freelance designer to update your branding, delegating tasks will give you more time to focus on growing your business. Start small, hiring part-time or freelance help, until you can afford to hire full-time employees.

- **Upgrade Your Website or Ecommerce Platform**: As your business grows, your **website or e-commerce platform** may need an upgrade to handle increased traffic or sales volume. Investing in a **more scalable platform** like Shopify, WooCommerce, or BigCommerce can help you better manage orders, improve user experience, and reduce site crashes or downtime during peak traffic.

- **Advanced Analytics Tools**: Invest in **advanced analytics** to better understand customer behavior, marketing effectiveness, and overall business performance. Tools like **Google Analytics**, **Kissmetrics**, or **Hotjar** can help you gain deeper insights into how users interact with your site and products, allowing you to make data-driven decisions for growth.

- **Improve Product Quality**: Growth also means improving the **quality** of your product or service. Invest in improving your offerings based on customer feedback. Whether that's refining your product design, sourcing higher-quality materials, or enhancing your customer service, continuous improvement should always be part of your growth plan.

- **Financial Management Tools**: As your business grows, keeping track of finances becomes more complicated. Use **accounting software** like QuickBooks, FreshBooks, or Xero to manage expenses, track revenue, and generate financial reports. This will not only help you stay organized but also enable you to make informed financial decisions.

Identifying opportunities for growth is a key part of scaling your business. By exploring **additional revenue streams**, **expanding your target audience**, and **investing in more efficient tools and resources**, you create a solid foundation for sustained success. Growth requires both a mindset shift and strategic planning—so keep testing, learning, and adapting.

Remember, growth doesn't always have to mean drastic changes; it's often about making small, incremental improvements that compound over time. The more proactive you are in identifying and seizing opportunities, the quicker you can scale your business to new heights.

Build a Support System

Running a business can be overwhelming, especially when you're doing it alone. However, **building a support system** can make all the difference in maintaining your motivation, overcoming challenges, and growing your business. In this section, we'll explore the importance of **networking with other entrepreneurs**, **delegating tasks**, and **seeking mentorship or professional advice** to create a support system that propels you forward.

1. Network with Other Entrepreneurs

One of the most valuable aspects of being an entrepreneur is the ability to **connect with others who are on the same journey**. Networking with other entrepreneurs gives you access to a wealth of experience, insights, and potential partnerships that can help you grow your business.

- **Join Entrepreneurial Communities**: There are countless online and offline communities for entrepreneurs, such as **Facebook groups, LinkedIn groups, local meetups,** or industry-specific forums. Engaging with these communities helps you build relationships with like-minded individuals who can share advice, resources, and encouragement.

- **Attend Networking Events**: Attend **conferences, workshops,** and **business expos** where you can meet other entrepreneurs and industry leaders. Even virtual networking events can be highly valuable for connecting with peers who understand the challenges you're facing.

- **Collaborate on Projects**: Networking isn't just about exchanging business cards; it's about **building meaningful relationships** that can lead to collaborations. You might find opportunities to work on joint ventures, co-market products, or share resources. **Collaborations** can significantly boost your reach and help you access new markets.

- **Stay in Touch**: After meeting other entrepreneurs, don't let the connection fade. Follow up with emails, join their social media networks, or schedule a coffee chat to keep the relationship going. Building a network is a long-term investment that can yield returns for years to come.

- **Learn from Others' Experiences**: Every entrepreneur has gone through challenges—some of them are similar to yours. By networking, you can learn **from the experiences of others** who have faced and overcome the obstacles you might be dealing with. This can save you time and energy and help you avoid common mistakes.

2. Delegate Tasks Where Possible

As a busy entrepreneur, you don't need to do everything yourself. **Delegating tasks** is a crucial part of scaling your business and avoiding burnout. By handing off certain responsibilities, you can focus on the areas where you provide the most value and have the most expertise.

- **Identify Low-Value Tasks**: Take stock of all the tasks you perform regularly. Are there **repetitive** or **administrative tasks** that could be done by someone else? Whether it's managing social media, responding to customer inquiries, or processing orders, these tasks may not require your direct attention and could be handled by a **virtual assistant** or other specialists.

- **Outsource Specialized Tasks**: Consider outsourcing tasks that require **specialized skills** that you may not have, such as **graphic design**, **web development**, **accounting**, or **copywriting**. Freelance platforms like **Upwork, Fiverr**, or **Toptal** can connect you with talented professionals who can assist with one-time projects or ongoing work.

- **Hire Part-Time or Full-Time Help**: As your business grows, you may find it necessary to hire employees, whether full-time or part-time. **Hiring a team** to manage operations, marketing, customer service, or sales can help you scale efficiently. Be sure to prioritize hiring for roles that will free you up to focus on **high-impact activities**.

- **Use Tools to Automate**: Leverage **automation tools** to help with tasks that can be automated, such as email marketing, social media scheduling, or invoicing. Tools like **Zapier**, **Hootsuite**, or **Mailchimp** can automate processes, saving you time and energy.

- **Focus on Your Strengths**: By delegating tasks that aren't your strengths, you free up mental space to focus on what you do best. Whether it's product development, business strategy, or customer relationship-building, your time is better spent working on areas that contribute directly to your business growth.

3. Seek Mentorship or Professional Advice

No entrepreneur is an island. Even if you're doing well, seeking **mentorship or professional advice** can help you avoid common pitfalls and accelerate your growth. A mentor or advisor can provide **guidance, perspective,** and **expertise** that might be difficult to access otherwise.

- **Find a Mentor:** Look for someone who has been where you want to go—someone with experience in **starting and scaling businesses.** A mentor can give you **actionable advice** and **insight into industry trends,** as well as offer emotional support during challenging times. You can find mentors through **business organizations, entrepreneurial networks,** or **online communities.**

- **Join a Mastermind Group:** A **mastermind group** is a collection of entrepreneurs who meet regularly to share experiences, offer feedback, and solve problems together. These groups can help you gain new perspectives and hold you accountable for your goals. Being in a mastermind group allows you to **collaborate with others** who are also striving for success.

- **Consult with Professionals:** For specific areas like **legal matters, tax planning,** or **business strategy,** consider seeking **professional advice** from experts. Hiring a business coach, accountant, or lawyer can provide clarity and confidence when making important decisions.

- **Leverage Online Resources**: If you don't have access to one-on-one mentorship or advisors, use online resources like **business podcasts, YouTube channels**, or **online courses** to continue learning and growing. Many entrepreneurs share their expertise for free, offering valuable lessons on everything from marketing to personal development.

- **Be Open to Feedback**: Whether from a mentor, consultant, or network, be open to **constructive feedback**. Getting an outside perspective can help you see blind spots in your business and challenge your assumptions, ultimately leading to better decision-making.

Building a support system is essential for your success as an entrepreneur. By **networking with other entrepreneurs, delegating tasks**, and **seeking mentorship or professional advice**, you surround yourself with the right resources and people who can help you overcome challenges and capitalize on opportunities.

Remember that entrepreneurship is rarely a solo endeavor. Whether through **collaboration, outsourcing,** or **guidance,** leaning on others will allow you to focus on your strengths and keep your business growing.

"...connect with others who are on the same journey."

Prepare for the Next Level

As your business grows, it's essential to be proactive and **prepare for the next level** of success. This doesn't just mean scaling in terms of revenue—it involves getting ready to handle **increased demand, refining your offerings** based on feedback, and **updating your business plan** to reflect new goals and strategies. In this section, we'll explore how to plan for growth effectively and ensure that your business is prepared for whatever comes next.

1. Plan for Increased Demand

As you attract more customers and your business gains traction, it's likely that demand for your products or services will increase. **Planning for increased demand** is essential to maintaining quality, meeting deadlines, and avoiding bottlenecks.

- **Assess Your Current Capacity**: Take stock of your current systems, processes, and resources. Are you currently able to meet demand without compromising quality or service? Identify any **weak points** in your business operations that might need improvement as you grow. This could include inventory management, customer support, or production capacity.

- **Scale Your Operations**: Start **scaling your operations** by investing in tools, equipment, or resources that will help you manage a larger volume of orders or customers. For instance, if your business relies on manual processes, look into **automating tasks** or **outsourcing** specific functions. If you're running an e-commerce business, ensure your **website** and **checkout process** can handle higher traffic without crashing.

- **Build a Supply Chain That Can Scale**: If you're selling physical products, it's important to evaluate your **supply chain**. Can your suppliers keep up with increased demand? Are you prepared for longer lead times or potential supply chain disruptions? Build relationships with multiple suppliers, or look into warehousing solutions to ensure you can maintain consistent stock levels.

- **Prepare Your Customer Support**: With increased demand, your **customer support** needs will also grow. Be prepared to handle more customer inquiries by training additional staff, using **chatbots** for instant support, or creating a **robust FAQ page**. The quicker and more efficiently you can address customer concerns, the better their experience will be.

- **Optimize for Scalability**: Whether it's upgrading your website, expanding your social media presence, or improving your back-end processes, focus on optimizing every part of your business for **scalability**. The more efficient and automated your operations are, the easier it will be to handle an uptick in demand.

2. Refine Your Offerings Based on Feedback

As you grow, it's crucial to continuously **refine your offerings** based on customer feedback and market trends. Regularly **evolving your product or service** ensures that you stay relevant and competitive as your business expands.

- **Collect Customer Feedback Regularly**: Make gathering **customer feedback** a regular part of your process. Use surveys, reviews, or social media interactions to learn about your customers' experiences and preferences. Tools like **SurveyMonkey** or **Google Forms** can make it easy to collect and analyze feedback. This will help you understand what's working well and where improvements can be made.

- **Iterate on Your Products or Services**: Once you have a clear understanding of customer needs, make adjustments to your offerings accordingly. Whether it's improving the design of a product, adding new features, or altering your service delivery model, use the feedback to drive **continuous improvement**. Keep your product or service aligned with your audience's evolving desires.

- **Test New Ideas**: Experiment with new variations or additions to your current offerings. For example, you could introduce new pricing tiers, launch complementary products, or offer different service packages. Use A/B testing or pilot programs to test new ideas with a small group of customers before rolling them out more broadly.

- **Monitor Market Trends**: Stay informed about **industry trends** and **market shifts** to ensure your business adapts to changes in demand. Is there a growing trend in your sector that you can capitalize on? Are there new technologies, tools, or methods that can help you improve efficiency or customer satisfaction? Keeping your finger on the pulse of your industry allows you to stay ahead of the curve.

- **Refine Your Messaging**: As you refine your offerings, make sure your marketing and messaging reflect these changes. Be clear with your customers about how your products or services have evolved and why they should care. Update your **website, social media profiles,** and **advertising materials** to showcase any improvements or new features.

3. Update Your Business Plan

As your business evolves, so should your **business plan**. Updating your business plan is a vital exercise that ensures your goals, strategies, and metrics align with your current stage of growth and the direction you want to take your business.

- **Revise Your Goals**: Reflect on the goals you set in the early stages of your business. Are they still relevant? Have you achieved them? Based on where you are now, **set new goals** that are aligned with the next stage of growth. These could include financial goals, customer acquisition targets, or product development milestones.

- **Adjust Your Financial Projections**: Update your **financial projections** based on your new goals and anticipated demand. This includes revisiting your revenue forecasts, profit margins, and expenses. Ensure that your projections account for any **increased operational costs** (such as hiring staff or purchasing more inventory) as well as potential **investments** in marketing or technology.

- **Revisit Marketing and Sales Strategies**: As you expand, your **marketing strategy** should evolve to target a broader audience or adopt new channels. Review the strategies you've been using—are they still effective? Perhaps it's time to allocate more resources to digital marketing, or explore new forms of **advertising** or **partnerships**. Adjust your approach based on where you see the most potential for growth.

- **Reevaluate Your Team and Resources**: Your team and resources will need to scale along with your business. Are you prepared to expand your team to meet new challenges? Do you need to bring in new skill sets or hire additional support staff? Updating your business plan should include an honest assessment of the resources you need to support your growth.

- **Update Milestones and Timelines**: Set new **milestones** and **timelines** for your next phase of growth. Break down large goals into smaller, actionable tasks, and determine a realistic timeline for each. This will help keep you focused and ensure that you have a clear roadmap for the future.

Preparing for the next level of your business is about more than just growing your revenue—it's about being strategic and proactive in scaling your operations. By **planning for increased demand, refining your offerings based on feedback,** and **updating your business plan,** you'll position your business for sustainable growth and continued success.

As you look ahead, stay agile, open to feedback, and committed to improvement. The business landscape will continue to evolve, and your ability to adapt and plan for the next stage will determine your long-term success.

Maintaining Work-Life Balance

Prioritize Time Management

Effective time management is the key to maintaining steady progress without feeling overwhelmed, especially when you're balancing the demands of starting and running a business. To make the most of your time, you need to focus on consistency, efficiency, and eliminating distractions. In this section, we'll explore how to **stick to your 10-minute daily routine, batch similar tasks for efficiency,** and **use tools to automate repetitive processes**—all crucial strategies to maximize productivity with minimal stress.

1. Stick to Your 10-Minute Daily Routine

The foundation of this book is built on the idea of using just **10 minutes a day** to move your business forward. While it might seem small, these consistent, daily sessions add up over time, leading to big results.

- **Make 10-Minute Sessions Non-Negotiable:** Schedule your 10-minute work sessions at the same time each day so that they become part of your daily rhythm. Whether it's early in the morning before the day gets busy, during lunch, or in the evening, **stick to this routine** no matter how busy you are. Even on your toughest days, this small commitment will keep you moving forward.

- **Set Clear, Focused Tasks for Each Session:** Each 10-minute session should have a clear goal or task attached to it. Don't overcomplicate it—use this time to accomplish one simple thing, whether it's researching a competitor, writing an email, brainstorming ideas, or refining your business plan. Breaking things down into small, focused tasks will make them feel more manageable and less daunting.

- **Leverage the Power of Momentum:** Once you start working on a task, even for just 10 minutes, you may find it easier to keep going. The momentum you build over these short bursts of work often leads to increased focus and productivity throughout the day. If you have extra time, go ahead and continue; if not, simply pick up where you left off the next day.

- **Minimize Stress with Consistency**: One of the key benefits of sticking to a short, daily routine is that it helps you avoid overwhelm. By tackling small tasks each day, you're spreading out your workload in manageable chunks. This reduces the anxiety of having to "find time" for your business amidst your already busy schedule.

2. Batch Similar Tasks for Efficiency

When you're running a business, time is precious. **Batching similar tasks**—grouping related activities together—helps you save time and avoid the inefficiency of switching between different types of work.

- **Identify Task Categories**: Think about the types of tasks you regularly need to complete. Do you often need to write emails, update your website, or create content for social media? Group these tasks into categories like **communications**, **marketing**, or **administrative**.

- **Block Time for Each Category**: Instead of addressing tasks as they arise throughout the day, try **batching** them into specific time blocks. For instance, you might allocate 30 minutes every Monday morning to respond to customer inquiries and emails. On Tuesdays, reserve 20 minutes for social media posts or content creation. This allows you to focus on one type of task at a time, which improves concentration and reduces the mental effort needed to switch between tasks.

- **Optimize Your Workflow**: When batching tasks, think about how you can streamline the process. For example, if you're creating content for social media, you could plan and schedule posts for the entire week in one sitting. Use tools like **Buffer** or **Hootsuite** to schedule posts ahead of time, freeing up more time for other priorities.

- **Limit Distractions**: When you batch tasks, you can create a dedicated time slot to focus fully on that type of work, without constantly switching between different demands. This minimizes distractions and increases your overall efficiency. During these time blocks, eliminate any potential interruptions—put your phone on silent, close unnecessary tabs on your browser, and turn off notifications.

- **Be Realistic About Time**: As you batch tasks, be mindful of how much time each group of tasks will take. Avoid overloading yourself with too much in one batch, as it could lead to burnout. Start small, and over time you'll learn how to optimize your schedule to get more done without feeling rushed.

3. Use Tools to Automate Repetitive Processes

Automation is one of the best ways to free up valuable time and reduce the strain of repetitive tasks. By using the right tools, you can automate time-consuming processes, allowing you to focus on higher-value activities that move your business forward.

- **Email Marketing Automation**: Tools like **Mailchimp**, **ConvertKit**, or **ActiveCampaign** allow you to automate your email marketing campaigns. You can set up automated welcome sequences, product recommendations, and follow-up emails that run without you needing to manually send each message. This saves you time while ensuring that your audience stays engaged.

- **Social Media Scheduling**: Instead of manually posting to social media each day, use scheduling tools like **Buffer, Hootsuite**, or **Later** to plan and schedule your posts in advance. These tools allow you to create and schedule content for the week in one sitting, saving you hours each week.

- **Financial Automation**: Use tools like **QuickBooks** or **Xero** to automate bookkeeping tasks such as invoicing, expense tracking, and tax reporting. These tools can sync with your bank accounts to automatically categorize transactions and generate financial reports, so you spend less time managing your finances.

- **Customer Relationship Management (CRM)**: A **CRM tool** like **HubSpot, Zoho CRM**, or **Salesforce** can automate customer data management, lead nurturing, and follow-ups. By automating these processes, you can spend less time tracking leads and more time building relationships and closing sales.

- **Task Automation:** Tools like **Zapier** or **Integromat** allow you to automate tasks between different apps you use. For example, you can set up a "Zap" to automatically add new contacts from your email list to your CRM or create a task in your project management tool every time you receive an inquiry via email.

- **Order Fulfillment Automation:** If you run an e-commerce store, you can automate order fulfillment with services like **Shopify** or **BigCommerce**. These platforms can automatically calculate shipping, track inventory, and notify customers when their orders are shipped, reducing manual oversight.

Prioritizing time management is crucial for growing a business without burning out. By sticking to your 10-minute daily routine, batching similar tasks for efficiency, and using automation tools, you can maximize your productivity and stay focused on what matters most.

The key to time management isn't about finding more hours in the day—it's about making the most of the time you have. With these strategies, you'll be able to run your business more efficiently, reduce stress, and make consistent progress, even on your busiest days.

Take Care of Your Mental and Physical Health

As an entrepreneur, it's easy to get caught up in the whirlwind of building a business, but **taking care of your mental and physical health** is just as important as managing your business tasks. Without a healthy mind and body, you'll struggle to make clear decisions, stay focused, and maintain the energy required for long-term success. In this section, we'll explore how to **schedule regular breaks**, **practice stress-relief techniques**, and **stay active and eat well** to support your overall well-being and ensure that you can sustain your entrepreneurial journey.

1. Schedule Regular Breaks

Running a business can be all-consuming, and it's tempting to work nonstop to make progress. However, **working for long periods without breaks** leads to burnout, decreased productivity, and poor decision-making. **Taking regular breaks** is vital for maintaining focus, creativity, and mental clarity.

- **Use the Pomodoro Technique:** One of the most effective ways to incorporate breaks into your routine is to use the **Pomodoro Technique.** This method involves working for **25 minutes** followed by a **5-minute break.** After four Pomodoros (about two hours of work), take a longer break of **15–30 minutes.** This cycle helps prevent mental fatigue by providing frequent opportunities for rest and recovery.

- **Step Away from Your Workspace:** During your breaks, make a point to **step away from your workspace** completely. This gives your brain a chance to reset and rejuvenate. You might take a short walk, do a quick stretching routine, or even meditate for a few minutes. Physical movement during breaks is especially beneficial for improving circulation and reducing tension.

- **Use Breaks for Self-Care**: Treat your breaks as a chance to engage in activities that help you relax and recharge. Whether it's reading a book, practicing deep breathing, or enjoying a cup of tea, prioritizing **self-care** during breaks allows you to return to your work feeling refreshed and energized.

- **Set Boundaries**: While it's important to work diligently, it's equally important to set clear **boundaries** around your work hours. Avoid the temptation to work through breaks or extend your workday indefinitely. Scheduling regular breaks ensures that you can **maintain work-life balance**, keep stress levels in check, and prevent burnout.

2. Practice Stress-Relief Techniques

Entrepreneurship can be stressful, and the pressures of growing a business can sometimes feel overwhelming. That's why it's essential to develop **stress-relief techniques** to help you manage stress and stay calm under pressure.

- **Mindfulness and Meditation:** Mindfulness practices like **meditation, deep breathing,** or **journaling** are powerful tools for reducing stress and increasing mental clarity. Even just a few minutes a day can help you **refocus** and shift your mindset. Apps like **Headspace, Calm,** or **Insight Timer** offer guided meditation sessions that are great for beginners and busy entrepreneurs alike.

- **Breathing Exercises:** Deep **breathing exercises** are a simple but effective way to calm your nervous system and reduce stress. Try the **4-7-8 technique:** inhale for **4 seconds,** hold your breath for **7 seconds,** and then exhale for **8 seconds.** Repeat this cycle for a few minutes to help reset your stress levels. You can practice this anytime—before a meeting, when feeling overwhelmed, or before bed to improve sleep.

- **Gratitude Practice: Practicing gratitude** is another great way to alleviate stress. Take a few moments each day to reflect on what you're thankful for. Whether it's progress in your business, supportive friends, or personal growth, focusing on the positive can shift your mindset and help you approach challenges with a clearer perspective. Keep a **gratitude journal** or simply reflect on your day before you go to sleep.

- **Connect with Others**: Sometimes, just talking to someone who understands can ease stress. Whether it's a mentor, fellow entrepreneur, or friend, don't hesitate to **reach out for support**. Sharing your concerns and experiences with others can give you a fresh perspective and remind you that you're not alone in your journey.

- **Laugh and Have Fun**: Humor is a great way to relieve stress. Take a break to watch a funny video, listen to a podcast, or engage in any activity that makes you laugh. Laughter lowers cortisol levels (the stress hormone) and boosts mood, helping you feel more relaxed and focused.

3. Stay Active and Eat Well

Your physical health directly impacts your mental clarity, energy levels, and overall productivity.

Staying **active** and eating a **balanced diet** are essential for maintaining the stamina needed to run a business and stay focused.

- **Incorporate Movement into Your Day:** Sitting for long periods can lead to physical discomfort, fatigue, and decreased productivity. Try to **move regularly**—whether it's a 10-minute walk, stretching, or even a quick set of bodyweight exercises. If you're working at a desk, consider using a **standing desk** or an **exercise ball** to improve posture and engage your muscles.

- **Exercise for Energy and Focus:** Regular exercise boosts **endorphins** (the "feel-good" hormones) and enhances your overall energy and concentration. You don't need to commit to long hours at the gym; short, effective workouts like **HIIT** (high-intensity interval training), **yoga,** or even a brisk walk can make a significant difference in how you feel throughout the day.

- **Eat a Balanced Diet:** Nutrition plays a key role in mental and physical performance.

Eating a **well-balanced diet** that includes plenty of vegetables, fruits, lean proteins, healthy fats, and whole grains helps stabilize your blood sugar and provides sustained energy throughout the day. Avoid relying on caffeine or sugary snacks to power through; instead, opt for nutritious, energy-boosting snacks like **nuts, seeds,** and **fresh fruit**.

- **Stay Hydrated:** Dehydration can lead to fatigue, irritability, and lack of focus. Make sure you're drinking enough water throughout the day—aim for at least 8 cups (64 oz), or more if you're active. Keep a water bottle at your desk or workspace to remind yourself to stay hydrated.

- **Sleep Well:** Never underestimate the power of a good night's sleep. Sleep is critical for brain function, mood regulation, and overall health. Prioritize **quality sleep** by creating a relaxing bedtime routine, limiting screen time before bed, and ensuring your sleep environment is conducive to rest. Aim for

7-9 hours of sleep each night to feel refreshed and ready to take on the day.

Taking care of your mental and physical health is a crucial aspect of sustainable entrepreneurship. By **scheduling regular breaks, practicing stress-relief techniques,** and **staying active and eating well,** you'll ensure that you have the resilience and energy to continue pushing your business forward. Remember, taking care of yourself isn't a luxury—it's a necessity for achieving long-term success.

Reflect and Reset Regularly

Building a successful business is a dynamic process, and it's essential to **reflect and reset regularly** to stay on track. Over time, your goals, priorities, and personal circumstances may change. By taking time to reassess, adjust, and realign, you can ensure that you're not only making progress but also staying connected to the purpose that drove you to start your business in the first place. In this section, we'll explore how to **reassess your goals periodically, adjust your schedule to stay balanced,** and **keep your vision aligned with your values.**

1. Reassess Your Goals Periodically

Your business goals should evolve as your business grows and as you gain new insights. Regularly reassessing your goals allows you to stay agile and responsive to changes in the market, your personal life, and your business landscape.

- **Set Regular Checkpoints**: Make it a habit to assess your goals at least once a month (or more often, depending on your pace). During this time, ask yourself:
    - Are these goals still relevant?
    - Have any new opportunities or challenges emerged?
    - Am I still excited about my objectives, or do they need to be adjusted?
    - Have I achieved any milestones that require a shift in focus or strategy? These checkpoints provide clarity and help you stay connected to the bigger picture, even as the day-to-day tasks take over.

- **Break Down Long-Term Goals into Smaller Steps**: Long-term goals can feel overwhelming. To avoid burnout and maintain focus, break them down into smaller, achievable steps. For example, if your long-term goal is to grow your business to $1 million in revenue, break this down into quarterly milestones that are easier to track and adjust. Reassessing these smaller steps regularly helps you stay on course and make any necessary course corrections.

- **Celebrate Achievements**: As you reassess, take time to **celebrate what you've accomplished.** Even small wins are important for maintaining motivation and building momentum. By recognizing your progress, you reinforce your commitment to the journey.

2. Adjust Your Schedule to Stay Balanced

Entrepreneurship can demand a lot of your time, but without balance, it's easy to burn out. **Adjusting your schedule** periodically ensures that you're balancing work with rest and personal time, creating a sustainable workflow that you can maintain in the long run.

- **Review Your Time Allocation**: Take a step back and review how much time you're dedicating to various activities—work tasks, personal life, self-care, and family. Are you spending too much time on certain areas and neglecting others? Regularly adjusting your schedule allows you to ensure that all aspects of your life receive the attention they deserve. If your business is taking up more time than you intended, adjust your schedule to incorporate breaks, family time, or hobbies that recharge you.

- **Avoid Overloading Your Calendar**: It's tempting to fill your calendar with back-to-back meetings and tasks, but this can lead to burnout and frustration. Regularly reassess your **daily and weekly schedule** to make sure it's realistic and sustainable. If you find yourself overcommitted, don't be afraid to **say no** to things that don't serve your priorities. It's okay to protect your time and space.

- **Experiment with Time Blocking**: Time blocking involves dedicating specific periods of time to specific tasks. This helps you focus more deeply on each activity without being constantly distracted by new tasks. Experiment with **time blocking** your workday and adjust your blocks as needed to better fit your rhythm and energy levels.

- **Factor in Self-Care**: Make sure that self-care, exercise, rest, and personal time are non-negotiable parts of your schedule. Schedule these activities just as you would a business meeting or work task. Prioritizing self-care isn't selfish—it's essential for your long-term success.

3. Keep Your Vision Aligned with Your Values

Your business should be an extension of your values and vision. As you move through the day-to-day operations, it's easy to lose sight of your deeper purpose. Regularly reflecting on your **vision and values** helps you stay true to why you started your business in the first place.

- **Reconnect with Your "Why"**: Regularly remind yourself of the **vision** and **mission** behind your business. What inspired you to start this venture? What impact do you want to make in the world? Reconnecting with your "why" helps ground you when challenges arise and keeps you motivated during tough times.

- ○ Write down your mission statement or vision regularly to keep it fresh in your mind.

- ○ Reflect on how each decision you make aligns with your core values.

- **Assess Alignment with Your Values**: Over time, your values might evolve, or your business might shift in ways that no longer align with your original goals. Reflect on how your current business activities align with your personal values. If there's a mismatch, it may be time to make adjustments in your business operations, offerings, or target audience. For example, if you started your business to promote sustainable products but have found yourself increasingly focused on profit at the expense of environmental concerns, reassessing your approach may be necessary.

- **Stay True to Your Long-Term Vision**: It's easy to get distracted by short-term goals, trends, or pressure from others to pivot quickly. But remember that **true success is about staying aligned with your long-term vision.** When making decisions, ask yourself, "Does this align with where I want my business to go in the next 1, 3, or 5 years?" If it doesn't, it may not be worth pursuing.

Regularly reflecting and resetting your goals, schedule, and values helps ensure that your business stays in alignment with your true purpose. By reassessing periodically, you can stay flexible, avoid burnout, and build a business that feels rewarding both professionally and personally. Your journey as an entrepreneur is not just about growth—it's about growth in the right direction. Reflecting and resetting ensures you're headed where you truly want to go.

"...taking care of your mental and physical health is just as important as managing your business..."

CHAPTER 5

Launch Day and Beyond

Final Preparations for Launch

Can you hear the countdown? 10, 9, 8, 7, 6, 5...

This is coming together, you did it! All of your 10 minute sessions, excitement building, ideas you shaped into a plan, this is a beautiful thing. Please enjoy these moments, you are one of the fortunate ones who has started and will be launching a business.

...4, 3, 2, 1...Liftoff!!

Test All Systems and Processes

Before you officially launch your business, it's crucial to **test all systems and processes** to ensure everything works seamlessly. This testing phase allows you to identify any potential issues, troubleshoot problems, and ensure that your customers have a smooth and professional experience when interacting with your business. In this section, we'll explore how to **ensure your website is functional**, **verify payment systems**, and **check customer support readiness** to guarantee that everything is running as it should.

1. Ensure Your Website is Functional

Your website is often the first point of contact between you and your potential customers. A **well-designed, functional website** is crucial to establishing trust and professionalism. Testing your website ensures that users have a smooth and seamless experience, regardless of what device or browser they are using.

- **Test Across Multiple Devices**: Your website should be **mobile-friendly** and responsive across various devices, including desktops, laptops, tablets, and smartphones. Visit your website from different devices and browsers to check if everything is displaying correctly and if the site's functionality is intact. **Broken links, slow loading times**, and **misaligned elements** can frustrate visitors and cause them to leave without taking action.

- **Check for Navigation and User Experience:** Ensure your site's navigation is **easy to follow.** Visitors should be able to find what they need quickly. Test all key pages, including your **home page, product/service pages,** contact **information,** and **checkout process.** Make sure that all **buttons** and **links** are working, and that your content is easy to read and properly formatted.

- **Verify Forms and Contact Features:** If you have forms on your website (such as contact forms, sign-up forms, or lead capture forms), make sure they're **functional.** Test the form submission process to ensure that you're receiving the information correctly, and that visitors get a confirmation message after submitting.

If you're offering a newsletter or special offer in exchange for email sign-ups, verify that the opt-in process works smoothly.

- **Test Load Speed:** Website speed is a key factor in user experience and search engine rankings. Use tools like **Google PageSpeed Insights** or **Pingdom** to assess how quickly your website loads. Aim for **fast load times** (less than 3 seconds), as delays can cause users to abandon your site.

2. Verify Payment Systems Work Smoothly

If you're selling products or services online, ensuring that your payment systems are functioning properly is essential. Any hiccups in the payment process can lead to lost sales, customer frustration, and potential damage to your reputation.

- **Test Different Payment Methods:** Whether you're accepting payments via **credit card, PayPal, Stripe,** or another payment processor, it's important to test each method thoroughly. Simulate purchases using each payment option to ensure transactions go through without issues. This will help you spot any errors or delays in the payment process.

- **Ensure Security Measures Are in Place**: Customers want to feel confident that their personal and financial information is secure. Make sure your **SSL certificates** (the "https://" in your website's URL) are active, and that payment systems are set up with proper encryption. Testing these security features will help protect both you and your customers.

- **Review Checkout Process**: The checkout process should be simple and user-friendly. Test the entire flow, from adding items to the cart to finalizing the purchase. Make sure there are no hidden fees, that the order summary is clear, and that the confirmation emails are being sent correctly. If there are any barriers or confusing steps in the checkout process, it's better to identify and resolve them before launch.

- **Test Refunds and Cancellations**: If your business allows returns or cancellations, ensure that the **refund process** works smoothly as well. Test the process for issuing refunds, including verifying that customers are notified properly and that any relevant records are updated in your system.

3. Check Customer Support Readiness

Having effective customer support in place is essential for building trust and resolving issues quickly. Before your launch, make sure that your **customer support systems** are ready to handle inquiries and provide timely, professional responses.

- **Test Your Support Channels**: If you offer support via **email, live chat, social media,** or a **helpdesk ticketing system,** test these channels to ensure they are functioning correctly. Send test messages or inquiries to see how quickly and effectively responses are provided. You should be able to answer common questions promptly and accurately.

- **Ensure Availability and Response Times:** If you're running a solo business, it's still important to have clear expectations set for how quickly customers can expect responses. Even if you can't offer 24/7 support, set realistic **response time goals** and **communicate those** on your website or in automated messages. Customers will appreciate knowing when they can expect help.

- **Create an FAQ Section**: An **FAQ** section is a great way to address common customer questions and reduce the need for direct support. Review your website to ensure the **FAQ** is comprehensive and up-to-date. Test it by asking common questions that your customers might have and ensure they're addressed clearly.

- **Simulate Real-Life Scenarios**: Put yourself in your customers' shoes and simulate real-life scenarios. For example, try **returning a product** or **asking a common service question**. Evaluate whether the support experience is smooth, efficient, and helpful. Ensure that your customer service team is trained to handle inquiries professionally and with empathy.

Testing all systems and processes before you launch ensures that your business is ready for action. By making sure your **website is functional, payment systems work smoothly,** and **customer support is prepared,** you're setting yourself up for success and creating a positive experience for your customers from day one. Taking the time to iron out any issues before your official launch will not only save you headaches later but also foster trust and satisfaction among your audience.

Plan Your Launch Strategy

A successful business launch doesn't happen by accident—it's the result of careful planning and strategic action. Your **launch strategy** sets the tone for your business's initial success, and the way you introduce your business to the world can have a significant impact on its growth. In this section, we'll explore how to **announce your launch to your network, use email and social media campaigns,** and **offer limited-time deals** to attract attention and drive early sales.

1. Announce Your Launch to Your Network

Your **network**—whether it's friends, family, colleagues, or existing customers—is one of the most valuable assets you have when launching a business. These are the people who already know and trust you, and they can be your **first advocates.**

- **Craft a Compelling Announcement**: Start by creating an announcement that shares your **excitement** and **vision** for the business. Be clear about what your business offers and why it matters. Include a **personal story** behind the business, as this helps build an emotional connection with your audience. Make it **short, engaging,** and easy to share.

- **Leverage Your Existing Relationships**: Reach out to your network directly via **email, text messages,** or **personal calls.** Personal touches increase the likelihood of them sharing your business with their own networks. You might say something like, "I'm launching something I'm so excited about, and I'd love your support. Here's a special offer just for you." The key is to make your launch feel exclusive and personal to those who already know you.

- **Use Referrals and Word-of-Mouth**: Encourage your network to **spread the word** by offering them incentives such as early access, a **discount**, or a **special reward** for every new customer they refer. Word-of-mouth marketing is incredibly powerful, and it can jumpstart the growth of your business if you tap into your community's enthusiasm.

- **Set a Launch Date**: Give your network a specific **launch date** so they know when to expect your business to go live. This creates a sense of **anticipation** and **excitement**. You could even host a **virtual launch party** or an event that offers sneak peeks of your products/services.

₂. Use Email and Social Media Campaigns

To reach a larger audience and generate buzz, **email marketing** and **social media campaigns** are essential tools. These platforms allow you to directly connect with potential customers and drive engagement.

- **Build an Email List in Advance**: If you don't already have an email list, start building one as early as possible. Offer something valuable (like a **free e-book, discount,** or **exclusive content**) in exchange for people's email addresses.

Leading up to your launch, you can use your email list to **build anticipation** with teaser emails, countdowns, and sneak previews of what's to come.

- **Launch Email Sequence:** Create a **sequence of emails** leading up to your launch. These should be spaced out over several days or weeks and designed to generate interest and excitement. Here's a sample sequence you could use:

    - **Email 1 (Teaser):** "Something exciting is coming soon..."

    - **Email 2 (Story/Behind-the-Scenes):** Share why you started your business and what makes it unique.

    - **Email 3 (Launch Announcement):** Announce the official launch date, product details, and any special offers.

    - **Email 4 (Reminder/Last Chance):** Send a final reminder email about your launch or any limited-time deals.

- **Leverage Social Media Platforms**: Social media is a fantastic way to **engage with your audience** before, during, and after your launch. Choose the platforms where your target audience is most active, whether it's **Instagram, Facebook, LinkedIn, Twitter,** or **TikTok.**

  - **Tease the Launch**: Share **behind-the-scenes content**, sneak peeks of your products or services, and countdowns to create **anticipation**.

  - **Use Engaging Formats**: Use a mix of **posts, videos, stories,** and **live broadcasts** to keep your audience engaged. Video content, especially, can create a more personal connection with your followers and help build excitement.

  - **Hashtags and Trends**: Make use of **relevant hashtags** and engage with popular trends to get more visibility. Consider creating a **branded hashtag** specific to your launch so people can follow the excitement and share their experiences.

- **Collaborate with Influencers**: If applicable, **partner with influencers** or bloggers who align with your brand. Even micro-influencers with smaller followings can help amplify your reach and add credibility to your launch. Look for individuals who are genuinely excited about your product or service and whose followers align with your target audience.

3. Offer Limited-Time Deals to Attract Attention

Creating a sense of **urgency** is one of the most effective ways to drive immediate action. Offering **limited-time deals** or special incentives during your launch will not only attract attention but also encourage early purchases and customer loyalty.

- **Launch Discounts**: Offering a **discount** on your products or services for the first 24-48 hours can create a rush of sales. For example, you could offer **10% off** or even **buy one, get one free** for your first customers. Make sure to clearly communicate the **expiration date** of the offer to create urgency.

- **Exclusive Access**: Consider offering **exclusive access** to your products or services for early supporters. You might give them a **first look** at new products, **priority ordering**, or **VIP customer status**. This makes your early customers feel valued and builds a strong sense of community around your brand.

- **Bundle Offers**: Another effective launch strategy is to create **bundled packages**. Offer a **discounted bundle** that includes multiple products or services at a special price for a limited time. This not only encourages larger purchases but also introduces customers to a broader range of what your business offers.

- **Referral Bonuses**: In addition to offering deals to your direct customers, you can incentivize your existing network and early adopters to **refer others** by offering a bonus or reward for each new customer they bring in. This creates a viral marketing effect, spreading your brand through word-of-mouth.

A successful launch is all about creating excitement, generating awareness, and driving initial sales. By **announcing your launch to your network, using email and social media campaigns,** and **offering limited-time deals,** you'll not only attract attention but also lay the foundation for long-term success. Don't be afraid to get creative and think outside the box—you want your launch to be memorable and leave a lasting impression on your customers.

Set Launch Day Goals

The day you launch your business is a pivotal moment in your entrepreneurial journey. To make the most of it, **setting clear launch day goals** is essential. Without goals, it's easy to get lost in the excitement and forget to focus on measurable outcomes. By aiming for specific objectives and tracking key metrics, you can evaluate your launch's success and adjust your strategy moving forward. In this section, we'll discuss how to **aim for specific sales or sign-up targets, track engagement metrics,** and **gather initial customer**

feedback to ensure you're hitting the ground running.

1. Aim for a Specific Number of Sales or Sign-ups

Your launch day is the perfect opportunity to start generating sales or sign-ups and begin building momentum for your business. Setting a **realistic and specific target** for how many sales or sign-ups you want to achieve will give you a clear focus and keep you motivated.

- **Define Your Goal**: Based on your product pricing, expected conversion rates, and marketing efforts, set a **realistic number of sales** or **sign-ups** you want to achieve on launch day. For example, if you're offering a service, you might aim for 10 sign-ups in the first 24 hours. If you're selling a physical product, your goal might be to sell 50 units. Make sure the goal is ambitious but achievable given your current resources and audience size.

- **Track Real-Time Progress**: As the day progresses, keep an eye on your sales or sign-up numbers. Many website platforms, such as **Shopify** or **Wix**, allow you to track transactions in real time. Set up alerts so that you're immediately notified when someone makes a purchase or signs up. This can help you celebrate milestones along the way and give you a sense of accomplishment.

- **Incentivize Early Action:** Consider offering a special bonus or reward for the **first 10 customers** or the **first 50 sign-ups**. This can help drive urgency and encourage people to act fast, which can result in a surge of activity during launch day.

- **Be Flexible with Your Goals:** While it's important to aim for a specific number, be flexible with your expectations. Not every launch will hit the target right away, and that's okay. The goal is to create momentum and use the launch as a learning experience to refine your marketing and product offering.

2. Track Engagement Metrics

Your launch day is not just about the number of sales or sign-ups—it's also about how people are engaging with your brand. Tracking **engagement metrics** will give you valuable insights into how well your audience is responding to your marketing efforts.

- **Monitor Website Traffic:** Use tools like **Google Analytics** or your website's built-in analytics to track how much traffic your site is receiving on launch day. Look for spikes in traffic during key times (like when your email campaign goes live or when your social media posts go out). Tracking this data will help you understand which marketing channels are driving the most visitors.

- **Analyze Social Media Engagement:** Track likes, shares, comments, and mentions on social media platforms. Tools like **Hootsuite, Buffer,** or platform-specific insights can give you an overview of how well your posts are performing. Are people interacting with your content? Are they sharing it with their networks? High engagement can be a sign that your message is resonating and your launch is generating excitement.

- **Monitor Email Campaign Performance:** If you've sent out launch emails, track their

open rates, click-through rates, and **conversion rates.** Are people opening your emails? Are they clicking on the links you've included? These metrics will help you evaluate the effectiveness of your email strategy and determine if there are any areas for improvement.

- **Look at Referral and Affiliate Data:** If you're using **referral programs** or working with **affiliate marketers** to spread the word, track how many people are coming from those sources. Seeing where your traffic and conversions are coming from will allow you to double down on the most effective channels for future marketing efforts.

3. Gather Initial Customer Feedback

On launch day, it's important to start gathering **feedback** from your customers. Their insights will be invaluable as you refine your product or service and improve the overall customer experience.

- **Encourage Feedback in Real Time:** Use pop-up forms, surveys, or automated emails to ask customers for feedback on their experience. For example, after someone makes a purchase or signs up for your service, send them a quick email or survey asking about their experience and what they think of the product. Tools like **Google Forms**, **SurveyMonkey**, or **Typeform** are simple to set up and can help you collect feedback quickly.

- **Monitor Social Media Mentions**: Pay attention to what people are saying about your launch on social media. Are they excited? Do they have questions or suggestions? Engaging with your audience on platforms like Twitter, Facebook, or Instagram can provide valuable insights into how they feel about your business and help you address concerns or questions in real time.

- **Ask for Testimonials**: If you're getting positive feedback, ask customers if they'd be willing to provide a **testimonial** that you can use on your website or in future marketing materials. These early reviews can help build social proof and trust with future customers.

- **Offer Incentives for Detailed Feedback**: To encourage more thoughtful feedback, consider offering an **incentive** such as a discount on their next purchase or a special bonus for completing a survey. This can help you gather more in-depth responses that provide better insights into how you can improve your products or services.

Setting clear launch day goals gives you a roadmap for success and allows you to measure the impact of your launch. By aiming for specific sales or sign-ups, tracking engagement metrics, and gathering initial feedback, you can evaluate how well your launch is performing and make any necessary adjustments for future growth. Remember, launch day is just the beginning—use this data to continue refining your business and keep the momentum going!

Executing a Successful Launch

Stay Organized and Focused

Launch day can be a whirlwind of excitement and activity, but to ensure everything goes smoothly, it's essential to **stay organized and focused**. By sticking to your launch plan, monitoring progress throughout the day, and addressing any issues promptly, you can ensure that the day goes as planned and that you set yourself up for future success. Let's explore how to **maintain focus**, **stay organized**, and **respond to challenges quickly** as you bring your business to life.

1. Stick to Your Launch Plan

A well-thought-out launch plan is your roadmap to success, and it's important to stay on track throughout the day. While things may not go exactly as anticipated, having a clear **plan** ensures you stay organized and on top of your key tasks.

- **Prioritize Key Actions**: Before launch day, create a **timeline** of what needs to be done and when. This could include **sending launch emails**, posting on social media, checking the status of your website, and making sure your payment systems are working. On launch day, keep a list of the most critical tasks and focus on those first, especially during the high-traffic moments.

- **Allocate Time for Each Task**: Set **time blocks** for each major task, whether it's responding to emails, monitoring social media, or checking website traffic. Make sure you allocate enough time for each task but don't overcommit—keep your focus on the things that will have the most impact on your launch.

- **Delegate When Necessary**: If you have a team or helpers, be sure to **delegate tasks** to others to stay focused on the bigger picture. For example, if you have someone helping with customer service, let them handle inquiries while you focus on monitoring sales and engaging with your audience on social media.

- **Avoid Distractions**: Launch day is not the time to get sidetracked by non-essential tasks. Stay disciplined and avoid distractions that could derail your momentum. This means limiting time spent on personal matters or other unrelated tasks.

2. Monitor Progress Throughout the Day

Keeping track of how things are going during your launch is crucial to understanding your progress and identifying any potential problems. Real-time monitoring allows you to **make adjustments quickly** and stay ahead of any issues.

- **Set Up Alerts**: Use tools like **Google Analytics**, **social media dashboards**, and **email tracking** to get real-time alerts on sales, website traffic, or social media engagement. Having these alerts in place means you won't miss important updates, such as when a significant sale is made or when there's a spike in traffic.

- **Check Your Metrics Regularly**: Set aside specific intervals throughout the day to review key metrics. For example, check **website traffic** in the morning, **social media engagement** after lunch, and **sales or sign-ups** in the evening. This will allow you to spot patterns and identify any potential problems early. If you notice a dip in engagement or sales, it might be time to tweak your social media strategy or send a follow-up email.

- **Track Feedback:** In addition to metrics, monitor any customer feedback or issues. If customers are experiencing trouble with your website or payment system, it's critical to act quickly to fix the problem. **Customer satisfaction** should be a top priority on launch day, and the sooner you can address any complaints or concerns, the better.

- **Celebrate Wins, Big and Small:** Take time throughout the day to celebrate the small wins. Whether it's your first sale, your 10th sign-up, or a positive comment on social media, celebrating these milestones will keep your spirits high and remind you of the progress you've made. These little victories can keep you motivated and focused as the day progresses.

3. Address Any Issues Promptly

Launch day rarely goes without some hiccups, so it's crucial to be **prepared to address any issues** that arise. Whether it's a technical glitch, a customer service issue, or an unexpected delay, staying calm and acting quickly will help you resolve problems and keep your launch on track.

- **Troubleshoot Technical Problems**: If you run into any technical issues—such as website downtime, broken payment links, or checkout problems—make them a priority. Have a **backup plan** in place, such as a list of contact details for technical support or a checklist of steps to follow if things go wrong. If the issue is significant, it's okay to **pause** certain activities (like your email campaign or social media posts) until the problem is resolved.

- **Stay Calm and Solution-Oriented**: When issues arise, take a deep breath and remember that challenges are part of the process. Focus on solutions rather than dwelling on the problem. Identify the root cause of the issue and take steps to fix it, whether that involves **contacting customer support**, **updating a website feature**, or **managing a customer complaint**.

- **Communicate with Your Customers**: If a problem affects your customers (such as delayed shipping or issues with the checkout process), it's important to communicate openly and promptly. Send an **email update** or **post on social media** to explain the situation and offer solutions, such as a refund, discount, or alternative product. Keeping your customers in the loop builds trust and demonstrates that you're committed to resolving any issues.

- **Learn from Mistakes:** Every launch is a learning experience. If something doesn't go according to plan, take note of what went wrong and use it as a learning opportunity for your next launch. Be sure to review customer feedback and look for patterns to help you refine your processes and avoid similar issues in the future.

Staying organized and focused on launch day ensures that you're able to manage the excitement and keep things running smoothly. By **sticking to your launch plan, monitoring progress throughout the day,** and **addressing issues promptly,** you'll not only keep everything on track but also demonstrate professionalism and resilience in the face of any challenges. Remember, the goal is not perfection, but to move forward with confidence and learn as you go!

"...maintain focus, stay organized, and respond to challenges quickly..."

Engage with Your Audience

Building a strong relationship with your audience is crucial for long-term success, and launch day is the perfect time to start that connection. **Engaging with your audience** fosters trust, builds community, and creates a sense of excitement around your brand. By actively responding to comments and messages, sharing behind-the-scenes updates, and expressing gratitude to your supporters, you create a memorable experience that can turn first-time visitors into loyal customers. Let's explore how to engage meaningfully with your audience on launch day.

1. Respond to Comments and Messages

Engagement is a two-way street. It's not just about putting your message out there—it's also about **listening to your audience** and responding in real time. Launch day is your opportunity to make a lasting impression by being **present and interactive.**

- **Be Quick and Personal**: As comments and messages start rolling in, make an effort to respond quickly and personally. Whether it's a simple **thank you** for a comment or a **detailed response** to a question, engaging directly with your audience shows that you care about their experience and value their input. Even a short, genuine reply can have a big impact.

- **Address Questions and Concerns**: If people are asking questions about your product, service, or the launch process, respond promptly with helpful answers. This shows that you're knowledgeable and committed to providing excellent customer service. If there's a recurring question, consider addressing it in a follow-up post or FAQ section on your website.

- **Engage on Multiple Platforms**: If you've announced your launch on several social media platforms or through email, be sure to check for comments and messages across all channels. It's easy to get caught up in one platform, but engaging on multiple fronts increases your visibility and shows that you're available wherever your audience is.

- **Use a Friendly, Authentic Tone:** People want to feel like they're communicating with a real person, not just a faceless brand. Use a **friendly and authentic tone** when responding. Humor, warmth, and empathy go a long way in building rapport and creating a positive experience for your audience.

2. Share Behind-the-Scenes Updates

Behind-the-scenes content is a great way to humanize your brand and offer a glimpse into the hard work and passion that went into your launch. People love to see what's happening "behind the curtain" and feel like they're part of your journey.

- **Share Your Launch Day Experience:** Post real-time updates about what's happening during launch day. Whether you're working through final preparations, celebrating early wins, or dealing with unexpected hiccups, sharing these moments with your audience helps them feel more connected to your story.

- **Highlight Team Members or Collaborators:** If you have a team or collaborators, highlight their contributions to the launch. Show your audience the faces behind the business, whether that's through photos, videos, or shout-outs in your posts. This not only adds a personal touch but also strengthens the sense of community around your brand.

- **Share Your Vision and Mission:** Reiterate why you started this business in the first place. Share the journey and the passion that drove you to create something new. When people understand the "why" behind your brand, they're more likely to connect with you on a deeper level. Whether it's a quick video message or a heartfelt post, this helps to create a **sense of purpose** that resonates with your audience.

3. Express Gratitude to Your Supporters

One of the most powerful ways to engage with your audience is by expressing **genuine gratitude**. Your supporters—whether they're early customers, family, friends, or followers—have helped you get to this point, and acknowledging their support can create strong emotional bonds.

- **Thank Your Early Customers**: If you've had customers purchase or sign up on launch day, be sure to publicly thank them on social media or through a personal email. This not only shows appreciation but also builds goodwill, encouraging them to spread the word about your business.

- **Acknowledge Your Community**: In addition to thanking individual customers, acknowledge the broader community that has supported you in your journey. This might include people who have shared your posts, offered advice, or even just shown moral support. Acknowledge their help and let them know how much it means to you.

- **Celebrate Together**: Invite your audience to celebrate your launch with you.

Whether you share a special milestone, offer a discount code, or host a live celebration, find a way to **share the joy** of the occasion. Making your audience feel like they're part of the celebration makes them more invested in your success.

- **Be Consistent in Showing Gratitude**: Gratitude shouldn't be reserved just for launch day—it should be a consistent part of your engagement strategy. Make it a point to regularly thank your audience for their support, whether it's a shout-out in a newsletter or a thank-you note in a product package. Gratitude goes a long way in building a loyal, engaged community.

Engaging with your audience on launch day—and beyond—creates a sense of connection, excitement, and trust around your brand. By **responding to comments and messages, sharing behind-the-scenes updates**, and **expressing gratitude** for your supporters, you humanize your business and foster a community that's invested in your success. These efforts don't just drive immediate results; they build long-term relationships that can lead to increased loyalty, word-of-mouth promotion, and sustained growth.

Evaluate Your Results

After the excitement of launch day begins to settle, it's time to **evaluate your results**. This step is essential not only for measuring the success of your launch but also for **learning from the experience** and setting yourself up for future growth. By comparing your outcomes to the goals you set, noting both successes and areas for improvement, and planning your next steps, you can continue building momentum and make data-driven decisions moving forward.

1. Compare Outcomes to Your Goals

The first step in evaluating your results is to **compare** the actual outcomes with the goals you set at the beginning of the launch process. This helps you understand what worked, what didn't, and where you need to adjust your strategy.

- **Review Key Metrics**: Take a look at the **metrics** you tracked throughout launch day, such as sales, sign-ups, website traffic, social media engagement, and customer feedback. Did you hit your sales or sign-up goals? How did your engagement numbers compare to expectations? Be honest with yourself and assess whether your goals were realistic or if you need to adjust them for future launches.

- **Evaluate Conversion Rates**: If you were tracking conversions—whether from a website visitor to a customer or from an email subscriber to a paid user—take note of your **conversion rates**. A high conversion rate may indicate that your messaging and call-to-action were on target. If the conversion rate was lower than expected, try to identify why—was there a technical issue, a misalignment in your marketing messaging, or a disconnect between the traffic you attracted and your target audience?

- **Reflect on Your Launch Plan**: Look back at the launch plan you created. Were you able to stick to it and accomplish the tasks you set out to do? If something was missed or didn't go as planned, take note so that you can adjust your approach for the next time. Maybe you overestimated how much time certain tasks would take, or perhaps you found new tasks that should be added to the plan.

2. Note Successes and Areas for Improvement

Reflecting on both **successes** and **areas for improvement** is crucial for growth. No launch will be perfect, but every launch offers valuable learning opportunities. By taking a balanced approach to self-assessment, you can celebrate your wins while identifying the changes that will help you improve next time.

- **Celebrate What Went Well**: Start by recognizing the successes, both big and small. Did you get more sign-ups or sales than you anticipated? Was your social media strategy effective? Did you receive positive feedback from early customers? Acknowledge your wins—this will keep you motivated and remind you of the progress you've made. It's also important to recognize the efforts that led to these successes, whether it was your marketing strategy, customer service, or the quality of your product.

- **Identify Areas for Improvement**: Now, turn your attention to the aspects that didn't go as planned. Did your website crash or experience technical glitches? Did you fail to generate as much traffic as you hoped? Were there delays or issues with customer service? Be honest about where things fell short, but avoid being overly critical. **Pinpoint specific areas**—whether that's a technical issue, a marketing gap, or a missed opportunity—and make a note of what you can do to improve in the future.

- **Ask for Feedback**: In addition to your own reflections, ask for **feedback** from your customers, team members, or peers. What did they think went well? What could have been done differently? This external input can give you new perspectives and highlight areas you might have missed in your own assessment.

3. Plan Your Next Steps

Once you've evaluated your results, it's time to use that information to **plan your next steps**. This is where you'll turn your reflections into action and adjust your strategy for future growth.

- **Adjust Your Strategy**: Based on what you've learned, make any necessary adjustments to your overall business or marketing strategy. If you didn't hit your traffic or sales goals, consider revising your marketing efforts or testing new strategies for lead generation. If certain customer pain points became evident, think about how you can adjust your product or service to better meet their needs.

- **Set New Goals**: Now that you have real data to work with, it's time to set new, **informed goals** for your next phase of growth. Perhaps you want to aim for a higher conversion rate, a broader social media reach, or a more efficient sales funnel. Use your initial launch as a foundation for setting these goals and ensure that they're **specific**, **measurable**, and **achievable**.

- **Create an Action Plan**: With your new goals in mind, create an **action plan** for how you'll achieve them. Break down the steps into manageable tasks that you can accomplish day by day, and incorporate these into your ongoing 10-minute-a-day routine. Whether it's improving your website, tweaking your marketing copy, or building out your customer service process, each small action will move you closer to your long-term goals.

- **Celebrate and Reset**: After you've reviewed your progress and planned your next steps, take time to **celebrate** your efforts and achievements. Even if everything didn't go as planned, the fact that you launched is a huge accomplishment! Reset your mindset, learn from the experience, and get ready for the next phase.

Evaluating your results helps you measure success, identify areas for improvement, and plan your next steps for growth. By comparing outcomes to your goals, acknowledging both your wins and challenges, and planning action steps based on what you've learned, you're setting yourself up for continued success. Every launch, no matter how big or small, is a step forward in your journey as an entrepreneur. Use the insights gained to refine your business, adjust your strategies, and stay focused on your long-term vision.

Sustaining Your Business Post-Launch

Keep Refining Your Processes

The journey of launching a business doesn't end after the initial excitement of launch day—it's an ongoing process of **refinement and improvement**. To build a sustainable and scalable business, you must continuously **refine your processes**, adjust your strategies based on feedback, and stay ahead of industry trends. This ongoing evolution will help you maintain momentum, stay competitive, and consistently deliver value to your customers. Here's how to keep refining your processes to ensure ongoing growth and success.

1. Implement Feedback from Customers

Your customers are one of your most valuable sources of insight. Whether they're sharing positive feedback or constructive criticism, listening to your customers will allow you to **improve your products, services, and overall customer experience.**

- **Act on Customer Suggestions**: When customers suggest improvements or express frustrations, treat this feedback as a gift. If multiple customers are asking for a specific feature or reporting the same issue, it's a sign that there's an opportunity for improvement. Prioritize addressing these pain points and let your customers know that you've listened and acted upon their feedback.

- **Follow Up with Customers**: After implementing changes based on feedback, don't forget to **follow up** with your customers. Let them know that their input helped shape your business. Not only does this reinforce customer loyalty, but it also shows that you value their opinion, which can enhance their overall experience with your brand.

- **Conduct Regular Surveys**: Even after launch, continue to collect customer feedback through **surveys, polls,** or direct outreach. These tools provide a simple way to gather actionable insights on a regular basis, and can guide your next steps for product improvements or service enhancements.

2. Regularly Review and Update Your Strategy

What worked for you at launch may not be as effective as you grow. Your business environment, customer preferences, and even your personal goals may shift over time. To stay ahead, you need to regularly **review and update** your business strategy.

- **Set Regular Checkpoints**: Schedule **quarterly** or **monthly reviews** of your strategy, goals, and processes. These reviews help you stay aligned with your vision while adapting to changes in the market or your business. During these sessions, assess the progress you've made, check key performance indicators (KPIs), and identify any areas of weakness.

- **Evaluate Your Marketing and Sales Tactics**: Your initial marketing approach may have been effective for launch, but as your customer base grows, your tactics may need to evolve. Review which marketing channels are driving the best results and consider experimenting with new strategies. For example, if you initially relied on organic social media growth, consider adding paid ads or influencer partnerships as your budget allows.

- **Refine Operational Processes**: As you start scaling, your internal processes will need to become more efficient. Look for ways to streamline operations, reduce manual work, and **automate tasks.** Evaluate everything from inventory management to customer service workflows and find areas where you can create smoother, more scalable systems.

- **Adjust Your Goals and Targets**: As your business matures, so should your goals. Review your original targets and adjust them as necessary to reflect your current business environment. If you've exceeded your initial expectations, it might be time to set more ambitious goals, whereas if you're facing challenges, it may require recalibrating your approach to hit more achievable targets.

3. Stay Informed on Industry Trends

To stay competitive, it's essential to keep your finger on the pulse of your industry. Being aware of **emerging trends, new technologies,** and **shifts in customer behavior** can give you a significant advantage over competitors.

- **Read Industry Blogs and Reports:** Stay up to date with the latest news by reading relevant **industry blogs, trade publications,** and **market research reports.** These resources provide insights into what's happening in your sector and can help you anticipate changes in consumer demand or identify new opportunities.

- **Attend Conferences and Webinars:** Whether virtual or in-person, attending industry conferences, webinars, or networking events can help you **expand your knowledge,** meet potential collaborators, and get ideas for innovation. Many events feature expert speakers and panel discussions that can help you stay informed on trends and best practices.

- **Follow Thought Leaders and Influencers:** Keep an eye on thought leaders and influencers in your field. Following them on social media or reading their books can provide valuable insights on how the industry is evolving. They often share tips, predictions, and examples of what's working in the market.

- **Conduct Competitor Analysis**: Regularly evaluate your competitors to see what they're doing well and where they might be falling short. By staying aware of what your competitors are offering, you can spot gaps in the market or areas where you can differentiate your business.

Refining your processes is an ongoing task that requires dedication, flexibility, and a commitment to continuous improvement. By **implementing feedback from customers, regularly reviewing your strategy**, and **staying informed on industry trends**, you position yourself to adapt quickly to changes and remain competitive in a dynamic business environment. Remember, growth and innovation aren't one-time tasks—they're part of your ongoing journey as an entrepreneur. By staying proactive and open to change, you'll set yourself up for long-term success and continuous business evolution.

Maintain Strong Customer Relationships

Building a successful business is not just about attracting customers—it's about **maintaining strong, lasting relationships** with them. Cultivating these relationships is crucial for encouraging repeat business, turning customers into brand advocates, and creating a sense of loyalty that can fuel your long-term success. In this section, we'll explore how to effectively **follow up with new customers, offer ongoing support and resources**, and **encourage repeat business**.

1. Follow Up with New Customers

The first impression you make on a customer is vital, but your follow-up is what solidifies the relationship and keeps them coming back. Following up after a purchase or interaction shows that you care and are committed to providing an excellent customer experience.

- **Send Thank-You Messages**: After a customer makes a purchase or signs up for your service, send a personalized **thank-you message**. Whether it's through email, text, or a handwritten note, expressing your gratitude reinforces the value of their decision to support your business. Let them know you appreciate their business and are excited to continue serving them.

- **Request Feedback Early**: A few days after their purchase or interaction, ask for **feedback** on their experience. This could be through a simple survey or a follow-up email. Not only does this show that you value their opinion, but it also provides you with valuable insights into how you can improve your products or services.

- **Offer Additional Information**: For customers who have made a purchase, provide **useful information** that enhances their experience with your product or service. This could include user guides, helpful tips, or related resources. This additional value helps to establish you as a helpful and knowledgeable business, not just a one-time transaction.

2. Offer Ongoing Support and Resources

Customer relationships don't end after the first sale. In fact, offering **ongoing support** and

resources helps keep your customers engaged and satisfied over the long term.

- **Create a Support System**: Whether it's through **customer service channels**, an online **help center**, or a dedicated FAQ section on your website, ensure your customers know that they can easily reach out for support. Responding promptly and offering solutions to their problems creates trust and loyalty, encouraging them to come back in the future.

- **Offer Educational Content**: Continuing to provide **valuable content** that helps your customers succeed with your product or service is a great way to strengthen relationships. Create **tutorials, how-to videos**, or **articles** that demonstrate new ways to use your offerings or solve common problems. By educating your customers, you show that you care about their success, not just their purchase.

- **Set Up a Loyalty Program**: Consider implementing a **loyalty program** that rewards customers for continued business. Offering discounts, exclusive products, or points for future purchases incentivizes customers to return and make repeat purchases. It also provides a sense of exclusivity that strengthens their connection to your brand.

- **Stay Available and Accessible:** Make sure your customers know they can always count on you. Whether it's through a **live chat feature**, email, or phone support, providing ongoing accessibility to answer questions or address concerns keeps your customers feeling cared for.

3. Encourage Repeat Business

Encouraging repeat business is one of the most effective ways to build a sustainable business. It costs less to retain an existing customer than to acquire a new one, so it's essential to have strategies in place to keep customers coming back.

- **Offer Special Deals for Return Customers:** One of the best ways to encourage repeat business is through **exclusive offers** for customers who've already made a purchase. You could offer a **discount on their next order**, special bundles, or an early access offer on new products. These deals give your customers a reason to come back while also showing your appreciation for their loyalty.

- **Create a Subscription or Membership Program**: If applicable to your business model, consider creating a **subscription** or **membership** program that offers ongoing value. This could be a monthly service, a subscription box, or access to exclusive content. Subscriptions not only ensure repeat business but also help stabilize your revenue streams.

- **Personalize the Customer Experience**: Use the data you've gathered from your customers to **personalize their experience**. This could mean sending tailored product recommendations based on their previous purchases or offering discounts on products you know they're interested in. Personalization makes customers feel seen and valued, increasing the likelihood of repeat purchases.

- **Stay in Touch**: Don't let your customers forget about you. Stay connected through regular **email updates, newsletters,** and social media engagement. Use these touchpoints to keep customers informed about new products, promotions, and company news. The more often you appear in their inboxes or feeds, the more likely they are to make another purchase.

Maintaining strong customer relationships is key to fostering long-term business success. By following up with new customers, offering ongoing support, and encouraging repeat business, you create a **loyal customer base** that will help propel your growth. Remember, it's not just about the sale—it's about creating an **experience** that makes customers want to come back again and again. A well-nurtured relationship can turn first-time buyers into lifelong advocates for your brand.

Look Forward to Your Next Milestone

As you progress in your entrepreneurial journey, it's important to keep your eyes on the **next milestone.** While celebrating your current achievements is vital, looking ahead and setting new long-term goals ensures that you continue to grow and push forward. This section explores how to **set long-term growth objectives, celebrate your entrepreneurial journey**, and **inspire others** by sharing your story.

1. Set Long-Term Growth Objectives

Every business needs a clear vision for the future. While short-term goals like launches or sales targets are crucial, **long-term growth objectives** help guide your business toward sustainable success. These objectives should align with your broader vision and mission, keeping you focused on building a business that lasts.

- **Define Your Future Vision**: Think about where you want to be in **1, 3, or 5 years**. What are the big-picture goals that excite you? Do you want to expand to new markets, introduce new products, or scale your operations? Your **long-term objectives** should challenge you to think beyond the day-to-day operations and encourage you to build a business that evolves over time.

- **Create Achievable Milestones**: Break down your long-term vision into **achievable milestones**. For example, if your goal is to double your revenue over the next two years, set interim milestones to track progress—such as increasing customer retention by 10% each quarter or launching one new product by the end of the year. These smaller wins keep you motivated and on track as you work toward your larger goals.

- **Plan for Scaling**: As you think about long-term growth, consider what scaling your business might look like. This could involve expanding your team, investing in new technology or systems, or increasing your marketing reach. Scaling often requires an investment of both time and resources, so plan accordingly and ensure that your business is ready for growth when the time comes.

2. Celebrate Your Entrepreneurial Journey

The road to entrepreneurship is filled with ups and downs, but every step forward deserves recognition. Taking time to **celebrate** your **journey**—not just the destination—helps you appreciate the progress you've made and reinforces the passion and drive that got you here in the first place.

- **Acknowledge Your Progress**: Take a moment to reflect on how far you've come. Celebrate the **milestones** you've hit—whether that's reaching a revenue target, launching your first product, or securing your first customer. Every victory, no matter how small, is a testament to your hard work and perseverance.

- **Celebrate Your Team (or Yourself)**: If you have a team, celebrate your collective efforts. Share your successes with those who have supported you along the way. If you're a solo entrepreneur, take a moment to acknowledge your own dedication and growth. You've chosen a challenging but rewarding path, and it's important to honor the journey as much as the destination.

- **Create Traditions**: Establish small, **meaningful traditions** for celebrating your progress. Whether it's a yearly retreat to review your goals, a quarterly team celebration, or simply treating yourself to something special after a major achievement, these traditions help reinforce the value of perseverance and celebration.

3. Inspire Others by Sharing Your Story

One of the most rewarding aspects of entrepreneurship is the ability to **inspire others**. Sharing your story—whether through blog posts, social media updates, or speaking engagements—can motivate and encourage other aspiring entrepreneurs who are just starting out or facing challenges in their own journey.

- **Be Authentic:** When sharing your story, be authentic and open about both your successes and your struggles. The most powerful stories are those that highlight the **real challenges** you faced and how you overcame them. Vulnerability creates connection, and your journey may resonate with others who are facing similar obstacles.

- **Offer Practical Advice:** As you reflect on your journey, share the **lessons** you've learned along the way. What would you have done differently? What tips do you have for people who are just getting started? Offering practical advice not only helps others but also positions you as a trusted voice in your industry.

- **Engage with Your Community**: Be an active part of your entrepreneurial community. Attend networking events, participate in webinars, and use your platform to share stories, advice, and encouragement. You never know who you might inspire or who might be inspired by you.

- **Celebrate Other Entrepreneurs**: Lastly, celebrate **others' successes** as well. Share the achievements of your peers, support fellow entrepreneurs in your community, and offer encouragement. When you lift others up, you build a community that thrives on mutual support and inspiration.

Looking forward to your next milestone is a natural part of the entrepreneurial process. Setting long-term growth objectives, celebrating your journey, and inspiring others through your story will not only help you stay motivated but also create a ripple effect that encourages others to take the leap into entrepreneurship. By looking ahead and continuously growing, you ensure that your business remains a dynamic and exciting venture—one that evolves with your vision and inspires those around you.

"...celebrate your entrepreneurial journey, and inspire others by sharing your story."

You're Off to Great Places

Persistence, determination and motivation are all key competencies for entrepreneurs and business owners. If you made it this far, congratulations! By now, you've taken crucial steps toward turning your entrepreneurial dream into a reality. You've crafted your business plan, mapped out financial projections, researched your audience and competitors, set up your systems, and started building relationships with customers. You've been disciplined in dedicating just 10 minutes a day to your business, and with each small step, you've laid a solid foundation for growth.

Let's recap the key steps you've taken:

Clarified Your Purpose: You've defined your mission, goals, and core offerings, ensuring your business has a strong foundation from day one.

Crafted a Simple Action Plan: You've broken down big tasks into manageable steps and created a clear execution plan with milestones, allowing you to move forward with confidence.

Validated Your Idea: By doing the necessary research and testing your idea in real-world conditions, you've ensured there's demand for your product or service.

Laid the Legal and Financial Groundwork: You've chosen the right legal structure, registered your business, set up financial systems, and budgeted wisely for your startup costs.

Focused on Marketing: You've created a professional online presence, developed your unique value proposition, and started building relationships with customers. You've leveraged low-cost marketing strategies to attract your audience and convert leads into loyal clients.

Committed to Continuous Improvement: You've embraced a mindset of progress over perfection, regularly reviewing your results and refining your processes to ensure ongoing growth.

Set Yourself Up for Success: With a clear action plan, a mindset for growth, and the resilience to face challenges, you're ready to thrive as an entrepreneur.

This is just the beginning of your exciting journey. While challenges are inevitable, remember that each step you take brings you closer to your ultimate goals. Keep focused, stay committed, and never underestimate the power of consistent, small actions. Your 10-minute daily commitment has set you on a path to success, and with every milestone you reach, you'll be reminded of the incredible progress you've made.

Thank You & Best of Luck!

I want to take a moment to thank you for taking the time to read this book and for investing in your entrepreneurial journey. The fact that you've completed this guide and are ready to take action speaks volumes about your drive and determination. I'm excited to see what you accomplish and confident that you'll make a positive impact with your business.

As you embark on the next steps of your journey, remember that entrepreneurship is about continuous learning, growth, and resilience. Keep pushing forward, stay open to feedback, and always be proud of the effort you put into building something meaningful.

Wishing you all the best on your business journey—may your success be as fulfilling as it is rewarding.

As a thank you for your support, I would like to offer you a surprise business gift to assist you. Please scan the code below from a mobile device to connect with me and claim your gift.

The QR code above will lead you to the following website:
https://mailchi.mp/e49730aa7f68/start-a-business-in-10-minutes-a-day

Your Feedback Matters

If this book has helped you, I'd be incredibly grateful if you could take a moment to **leave a review** on Amazon. Your feedback not only helps me improve but also encourages other entrepreneurs to take that first step. Share your thoughts on what you found helpful, your key takeaways, or how the book has impacted your journey. Your review will inspire others and help them navigate their own path to success.

Once again, thank you for your time, your dedication, and your commitment to your future. Best of luck, and I can't wait to hear about your progress!

Bonus - 100-Point Checklist to Launch a Business in 20 Days

Each day consists of 5 steps (5 days per week, 2 rest days per week), with each step designed to be completed in 10 minutes or less. Yes you can give yourself 2 days off a week to relax and have fun with family and friends!

Week 1: Foundation and Planning

Day 1: Define Your Vision

1. Write down your reason for starting this business.
2. Identify 3 personal goals you want to achieve..
3. Describe your target audience in one sentence.
4. Draft your mission statement.
5. Brainstorm potential business names.

Day 2: Research and Validate Your Idea

6. List 3-5 business ideas you're considering.
7. Research similar businesses online.
8. Identify 3 unique ways you could stand out.

9. Ask 5 friends or family members for feedback.

10. Choose one idea to pursue.

Day 3: Define Your Offerings

11. Write a simple description of your product or service.

12. Identify 3 main benefits your offering provides.

13. List any features that make your product unique.

14. Set a tentative price point.

15. Outline the problem your business solves.

Day 4: Plan Your Finances

16. Estimate your startup costs (tools, materials, etc.).

17. Research funding options if needed.

18. Identify potential revenue streams.

19. Set a goal for first-month earnings.

20. Create a simple budget.

Day 5: Map Out Your Action Plan

21. List all tasks needed to launch your business.

22. Break tasks into 10-minute steps.

23. Prioritize tasks based on urgency.

24. Assign deadlines to each task.

25. Organize tasks into daily themes.

Week 2: Building and Structuring

Day 6: Choose Your Business Name and Identity

26. Finalize your business name.

27. Check domain name availability.

28. Reserve your chosen domain.

29. Draft a tagline for your business.

30. Sketch or describe logo ideas.

Day 7: Create Your Business Structure

31. Decide on a legal structure (e.g., sole proprietorship).

32. Research registration requirements in your area.

33. Reserve your business name (if required).

34. List any licenses or permits needed.

35. Start the registration process online.

Day 8: Outline Your Business Plan

36. Write a one-page business plan.

37. Define your target customer persona.

38. Set short-term and long-term goals.

39. Describe your marketing strategy.

40. Outline a basic sales process.

Day 9: Develop Your Brand

41. Choose brand colors and fonts.
42. Create a rough sketch or brief for your logo.
43. Research free design tools like Canva.
44. Draft a simple brand style guide.
45. Test your branding with friends or peers.

Day 10: Build Your Online Presence

46. Create a basic website using a template.
47. Write an "About Us" section.
48. Add your product or service description.
49. Include contact information.
50. Ensure your website is mobile-friendly.

Week 3: Marketing and Preparation

Day 11: Set Up Social Media

51. Choose 2-3 social media platforms to use.
52. Create business profiles for each platform.
53. Add your logo and contact information.
54. Post an introductory message or video.
55. Invite friends to follow your pages.

Day 12: Prepare Your Marketing Materials

56. Write a short bio or elevator pitch.
57. Draft an introductory email template.

58. List 5 potential blog or video topics.

59. Create a simple flyer or brochure.

60. Plan your launch announcement.

Day 13: Engage Your Audience

61. Share your story about starting this business.

62. Post a question to spark engagement.

63. Join 1-2 online communities in your niche.

64. Comment on posts in relevant groups.

65. Respond to any feedback you receive.

Day 14: Finalize Your Product/Service

66. List any unfinished product details.

67. Test your product/service for quality.

68. Write instructions or FAQs for customers.

69. Create a refund or return policy.

70. Ask for feedback from 1-2 trusted people.

Day 15: Plan Your Launch Event

71. Choose a launch date and time.

72. Write a launch day checklist.

73. Draft a short launch announcement.

74. Create an event on social media.

75. Invite your friends and network to the launch.

Week 4: Launch and Post-Launch Activities

Day 16: Final Pre-Launch Preparations

76. Double-check your website for errors.
77. Test all payment methods.
78. Prepare a simple script for customer inquiries.
79. Review your social media schedule.
80. Confirm any collaborations or partnerships.

Day 17: Execute Your Marketing Strategy

81. Schedule posts for launch day.
82. Send your launch announcement email.
83. Share a countdown to launch on social media.
84. Engage with any responses or comments.
85. Reach out to local or online media.

Day 18: Launch Day

86. Announce your launch on all platforms.
87. Monitor your website and sales system.
88. Share behind-the-scenes updates.
89. Respond quickly to inquiries.
90. Thank your audience for their support.

Day 19: Post-Launch Follow-Up

91. Email a thank-you note to early customers.
92. Gather feedback through a simple survey.
93. Share testimonials on your platforms.
94. Review your launch day metrics.
95. Adjust your strategy for improvement.

Day 20: Plan for Growth

96. List 3 ways to expand your audience.
97. Set a goal for the next 30 days.
98. Identify 1-2 new product/service ideas.
99. Plan a small celebration of your achievement.
100. Reflect on lessons learned during the process.

References

Blank, S. G., & Dorf, B. (2020). *The Startup Owner's Manual: The Step-by-Step Guide for Building a Great Company* (2nd ed.). K&S Ranch.

Chesbrough, H. (2019). *Open Innovation: The New Imperative for Creating and Profiting from Technology.* Harvard Business Press.

Drucker, P. F. (2007). *Innovation and Entrepreneurship: Practice and Principles.* Harper Business.

Gerber, M. E. (2016). *The E-Myth Revisited: Why Most Small Businesses Don't Work and What to Do About It.* HarperCollins.

Bplans. (n.d.). *How to write a business plan.* Bplans. Retrieved January 10, 2025, from https://www.bplans.com/business-plan-template/

Forbes. (2023, July 15). *10 startup mistakes to avoid when launching a new business.* Forbes. Retrieved January 10, 2025, from https://www.forbes.com/sites/forbestechcouncil/2023/07/15/10-startup-mistakes-to-avoid-when-launching-a-new-business/

HubSpot. (2024, March 2). *How to create a business plan: A step-by-step guide.* HubSpot. Retrieved January 10, 2025, from https://blog.hubspot.com/marketing/how-to-write-a-business-plan

Inc. (2023, December 5). *The ultimate guide to marketing your startup in 2023.* Inc. Retrieved January 10, 2025, from https://www.inc.com/guides/startup-marketing-2023.html

Small Business Administration. (2024, January 9). *Choose your business structure.* U.S. Small Business Administration. Retrieved January 10, 2025, from https://www.sba.gov/business-guide/launch/choose-your-business-structure

Shopify. (2023, September 20). *How to build a brand: A beginner's guide for entrepreneurs.* Shopify. Retrieved January 10, 2025, from https://www.shopify.com/guides/build-a-brand

www.ingramcontent.com/pod-product-compliance
Lightning Source LLC
Chambersburg PA
CBHW030454210326
41597CB00013B/664